WOOD
HOLZ
BOIS

HOLZ | BOIS

WOOD

BARBARA LINZ

h.f.ullmann

Contents | Inhaltsverzeichnis | Sommaire

For some, the idea of building with wood calls to mind a traditional log cabin. However, modern conceptions of wood architecture and design tend to avoid the rustic and lean in the opposite direction.

Instead, strong lines, 90-degree angles and a regal impression determine the appearance. The focus, then, is not so much on the rustic raw material as on the intended use of forms that reveals itself in the finished product. Wood-trim strips, slats and splines bring striped patterns to the forefront. This attention to and emphasis on lines often coincides with the building's basic ascetic forms. Cubical buildings work well with austere facade designs and interior arrangements. The possibilities that present themselves here seem limitless.

Asian architecture already shows a long tradition of this understanding of raw materials. Modern Western wood architecture incorporates Asian style, for example, through the use of sliding wooden doors.

Many new, timely ideas for working with wood also come from other nations with a history of building with it, for example the Scandinavian and Alpine countries.

But wood is not only interesting with regard to surfaces; its building characteristics inspire architects: wood constructions per se are scaffold-like and are not massive - they seem light and open.

There are absolutely no limitations to specific building types in wood architecture. And, when considering specific demands, wood is sometimes the better choice. In this book, you will find four music buildings where wood is used because of its good acoustic qualities. Also interesting is the frequent use of wood in temporary architecture, such as exhibitions and fair pavilions. Such buildings appear almost as monumental sculptures.

And still, the reference to nature as our first dwelling, as the origin of all building and the source of creative materials that are both long-lasting and beautiful lives on in every wood design. Nearly all designers use the material unfinished, in its natural structure and color and its living aesthetic. Many of the buildings shown in this book use wood in a context of ecologically friendly buildings. Some of the architects use emphatically organic forms and not the linear forms described above.

Beim Thema Holzbau denkt manch einer an die traditionelle Blockhütte. Moderne Auffassungen von Holzarchitektur und -design vermeiden jedoch eher das Rustikale und tendieren in eine gegenteilige Richtung. Strenge Linearität und Rechtwinkligkeit sowie edle Ausstrahlung bestimmen stattdessen das Bild. Man bezieht sich dabei nicht auf den urigen Rohstoff, sondern vielmehr auf eine bestimmte Formensprache, die sich aus dem verarbeiteten Material ergibt. Holzleisten, -latten und -lamellen rücken Streifenmuster in den Vordergrund. Dieses Aufgreifen und Betonen von Linearität geht oft mit sehr asketischen Grundformen des Gebäudekörpers einher. Kubische Bauten lassen sich sehr gut mit einer strengen Grafik der Fassaden- bzw. Innenraumgestaltung verbinden. Die Variationsmöglichkeiten, die sich dabei eröffnen, scheinen unendlich. Dieses Verständnis des Werkstoffes hat in der asiatischen Architektur eine lange Tradition. Die moderne westliche Holzarchitektur greift den asiatischen Stil gerne auf – beispielsweise durch die Verwendung von Holzschiebetüren.

Aus anderen Nationen mit großer Holzbautradition, wie z. B. aus Skandinavien oder den Alpenländern, kommen allerdings ebenfalls viele neue, zeitgemäße Impulse für den Umgang mit dem Material.

Doch nicht nur im Hinblick auf Oberflächen ist Holz von Interesse; auch sein konstruktiver Charakter inspiriert die Architekten: Holzkonstruktionen sind per se gerüsthaft und nicht-massiv; sie wirken leicht und offen. In der Holzarchitektur gibt es grundsätzlich keine Beschränkung auf bestimmte Gebäudegattungen. Aber im Hinblick auf spezifische Anforderungen ist Holz manchmal die bessere Wahl. In diesem Buch finden sich alleine vier Musikgebäude, in denen Holz wegen seiner guten Klangträgereigenschaften zum Einsatz kommt. Interessant ist die häufige Verwendung von Holz in der ephemeren Architektur, als Ausstellungs- oder Messepavillon. Solche Bauten rücken in die Nähe von monumentalen Skulpturen.

Dennoch: Der Hinweis auf die Natur als unsere erste Behausung, als Ursprung jeglichen Bauens und als Quelle von Gestaltungsmaterialien von Dauerhaftigkeit und Schönheit, steckt wohl in jedem Holzdesign. Fast alle Gestalter nutzen das Material unverdeckt, in seiner natürlichen Struktur und Farbe und seiner lebendigen Ästhetik. Viele der in diesem Buch gezeigten Objekte verwenden Holz im Kontext ökologischen Bauens. Für einige Architekten sind dann betont organische Formen naheliegend und nicht die oben beschriebene Geradlinigkeit.

Pour certains, la construction en bois évoque une cabane en rondins traditionnelle, pourtant les conceptions modernes de l'architecture et du design en bois évitent tout ce qui est rustique, et tendent à prendre la direction opposée.

Leur esthétique est au contraire régie par des lignes fortes, des angles droits et une aura de noblesse. Le centre de l'attention n'est pas la matière brute, mais bien davantage le langage des formes, qui se révèle dans le travail des matériaux. Les frises, lattes et lames de bois mettent les motifs à rayures au premier plan. Cette idée d'une linéarité accentuée va souvent de pair avec des bâtiments aux formes de base très ascétiques. Les bâtiments cubiques se marient très bien avec les façades et les intérieurs au graphisme austère. Ces caractéristiques semblent admettre une infinité de variations.

L'architecture asiatique montre déjà une longue tradition de cette conception des matières premières. Aujourd'hui, l'architecture en bois occidentale reprend volontiers le style asiatique, par exemple à travers l'utilisation de portes coulissantes en bois.

D'autres pays qui possèdent une tradition solide de la construction en bois, par exemple les pays scandinaves ou alpins, sont la source de nombreuses idées nouvelles et contemporaines pour l'exploitation de ce matériau.

Mais le bois n'est pas seulement intéressant en tant que revêtement, ses caractéristiques structurelles inspirent les architectes : les constructions en bois s'apparentent à des échafaudages et, loin d'être massives, donnent une impression de légèreté et d'ouverture.

L'architecture en bois ne connaît absolument aucune limite quant aux types de bâtiment envisageables. Même lorsqu'il faut prendre en considération des demandes spécifiques, le bois est parfois le meilleur choix.

Vous trouverez dans ce livre quatre bâtiments consacrés à la musique où le bois est utilisé pour ses qualités acoustiques. Il faut également remarquer que le bois est fréquemment utilisé en architecture éphémère, pour des pavillons d'exposition ou de salons professionnels. Ces constructions s'approchent beaucoup de la sculpture monumentale.

On retrouve dans toute structure en bois la référence à la nature en tant que premier habitat de l'Homme, en tant qu'origine de toute construction et que source de matériaux de création architecturale à la fois beaux et durables. Presque tous les architectes utilisent ce matériau à l'état brut, avec sa structure et sa couleur d'origine et son esthétique vivante.

Beaucoup des exemples présentés dans cet ouvrage illustrent l'utilisation du bois dans un contexte de construction écologique. Certains architectes y associent des formes très organiques, et non les formes linéaires décrites plus haut.

PROJEKTE | PROJETS

PROJECTS

Lakeside Summerhouse

Because the building project is restricted by environmental-protection regulations, the architects from 24H have developed a house that can expand and retract: individual building elements are manoeuvrable. The similarity to a living creature catches the eye – a butterfly in its cocoon or an armadillo under its shell. "Dragspelhuset" (the accordion house) is the popular name for this building. The fact that the wood would develop a patina over time was taken into account. It is part of the naturalness of the building structure. A cladding made of clapboard is a local building tradition in Sweden (known as "stickor"), although in this case Canadian red cedar was used because the native soft wood is not suitable as an outer covering. To compensate, the whole interior is panelled with Swedish birch. Only environmentally friendly-certified wood was used and, along with the appropriate fixtures and fittings inside, the house has resulted in a building that is almost carbon neutral.

Sommerhaus am See

Weil Naturschutzauflagen den Baugrund eingrenzten, haben 24H-Architekten ein Haus entwickelt, das sich ausdehnen und zusammenziehen kann: einzelne Gebäudeteile sind beweglich. Die Ähnlichkeit mit einem Tier springt ins Auge – etwa mit einem Schmetterling im Kokon, oder mit einem Gürteltier. „Dragspelhuset" (Ziehharmonikahaus) ist der Spitzname des Objektes. Die sich mit der Zeit bildende Holzpatina wurde bewusst einkalkuliert. Sie ist Teil der Natürlichkeit dieses Baukörpers. Die Verkleidung mit Schindeln ist in Schweden lokale Bautradition („stickor" genannt). Umgesetzt wurde sie allerdings mit kanadischer Rotzeder, denn die heimischen Weichhölzer sind nicht für Außenverkleidungen geeignet. Dafür ist das Innere komplett in heller schwedischer Birke vertäfelt. Ausschließlich ökologisch zertifiziertes Holz wurde verwendet. Die Ausstattung des Hauses ergibt ein fast vollständig CO_2-freies Objekt.

Maison d'été au bord d'un lac

La surface constructible étant limitée par des lois sur la protection de la nature, les architectes de 24H ont imaginé une maison qui peut s'étirer et se contracter : elle comporte des éléments mobiles. On lui trouve immédiatement une ressemblance avec un animal, par exemple un papillon dans son cocon, ou un tatou sous sa cuirasse. Le projet a été surnommé « Dragspelhuset » (maison accordéon). La belle patine que le bois a acquise au cours du temps était prévue dès le départ. Elle fait partie du caractère naturel de ce bâtiment. Le revêtement de bardeaux est traditionnel dans l'architecture suédoise (« stickor »). Il est cependant composé ici de cèdre rouge canadien, car les résineux locaux ne conviennent pas aux revêtements extérieurs. En revanche, tout l'intérieur est tapissé de bouleau suédois clair. Tout le bois employé est certifié écologique, et la maison n'émet pratiquement pas de CO_2.

A covering made of wooden clapboard is so flexible it can follow the many curves of the building structure without any problem.

Eine Verkleidung mit Holzschindeln ist so flexibel, dass sie sich dem vielfach gewölbten Baukörper problemlos anpassen kann.

Le revêtement en bardeaux de bois est si flexible qu'il suit les contours des différentes voûtes du bâtiment sans aucun problème.

In the living and sleeping areas, reindeer pelts on the floor and ceiling add to the comfort.

Im Wohn- und Schlafbereich verleihen Rentierfelle am Boden und der Decke dem Innenraum Gemütlichkeit.

Dans le salon et la chambre, les peaux de rennes qui recouvrent l'intérieur du sol au plafond créent une atmosphère encore plus chaleureuse.

The old vacation house, on this site since the end of the 19th century, was retained and now nestles up to its new rustic companions.

Das alte Ferienhaus, das hier seit Ende des 19. Jahrhunderts steht, blieb erhalten und schmiegt sich nun an den urigen neuen Bruder.

L'ancienne maison de vacances, qui se dresse sur ce site depuis la fin du XIXe siècle, a été conservée et se blottit maintenant contre sa nouvelle compagne rustique.

Aequo

Eelde Barn House

A traditional building type was the model for the design of this residential construction – the classic peasant's barn from the Drenthe region. The new building is not a historical imitation but rather a structure that has been carefully designed to fit in with the existing architectural landscape while using new methods and a modern aesthetic. The minimalist exterior of the barn as a long, one-story gabled house with a smooth exterior and no roof overhang or wall projections was retained. The dominance of wood as building material was also preserved. The building is designed as a house within a house; a shell of red cedar surrounds the walls, doors and windows of the inner house. This shell consists of movable grids and is extremely flexible. The large gates act as window, door and sun-shade in one. They serve as screens integrated with the house that constantly reconfigure the surrounding terrace space.

Eelde Scheunenhaus

Ein traditioneller Gebäudetypus stand Pate beim Entwurf dieses Wohnhauses – die klassische Bauernhofscheune der Region Drenthe in Holland. Es handelt sich bei dem Neubau jedoch nicht um eine historisierende Imitation, sondern um eine behutsame Anpassung an eine vorgegebene Architekturlandschaft mit neuen Mitteln und moderner Ästhetik. Übernommen wurde die minimalistische äußere Form der Scheune als lang gestrecktes, eingeschossiges Giebelhaus mit glatten Außenflächen, ohne Dachüberstand oder Wandversprünge. Übernommen wurde auch die Dominanz des Baumaterials Holz. Das Gebäude ist als Haus im Haus konzipiert: Mauerwerk, Türen und Fenster des inneren Hauses sind umgeben von einer Hülle aus Rotzedernholz. Diese Hülle besteht aus beweglichen Gattern und ist extrem variabel. Die großen Tore sind Fenster, Tür und Sonnenschutz in einem. Sie strukturieren den Terrassenraum rings um das Haus stets neu und sind nutzbar als fest mit dem Haus verbundene Paravents.

Grange à Eelde

Cette résidence a été conçue sur le modèle de la traditionnelle grange de ferme de la région de Drenthe. Le nouveau bâtiment n'est cependant pas une imitation historique, il s'agit plutôt d'une structure soigneusement adaptée au paysage architectural existant grâce à des méthodes nouvelles et à une esthétique moderne. L'extérieur minimaliste de la grange a été conservé : un long bâtiment à pignon, sur un seul étage, avec des surfaces extérieures lisses et sans débord de toit ni ressaut des murs. La dominance du bois dans les matériaux de construction a également été conservée. Le bâtiment est conçu comme une maison à l'intérieur d'une maison : une coque de cèdre rouge entoure les murs, les portes et les fenêtres de la maison interne. Cette coque est composée de grilles mobiles et est extrêmement flexible. Les grandes portes sont de larges fenêtres dotées de stores. Elles font également office de paravents qui reconfigurent constamment l'espace de la terrasse qui entoure la maison.

The linear form of the wooden screens is repeated in the aluminum roof slats.

Das lineare Muster der Holzparavents wiederholt sich in den Aluminium-Dachlamellen.

Le motif linéaire de ces paravents en bois se répète dans les lames en aluminium du toit.

The blinds are essential for shade on the south side of the house, which has the largest window area.

Auf der Südseite des Hauses, die die größte Fensterfläche besitzt, sind die Gatterjalousien unverzichtbar als Sonnenschutz.

Sur le côté sud, qui présente la plus grande surface de fenêtres, les stores sont indispensables pour protéger la maison contre les rayons du soleil.

Bankirai hardwood floors inside and on the broad terrace areas create a seamless and extremely generous living area.

Holzböden im Inneren und breite Terrassenflächen aus Bankirai-Hartholz bilden übergangslos eine äußerst großzügige Wohngrundfläche.

Le bois dur de Bankirai établit un lien entre les sols de l'intérieur et de la grande terrasse, et crée une surface habitable extrêmement généreuse.

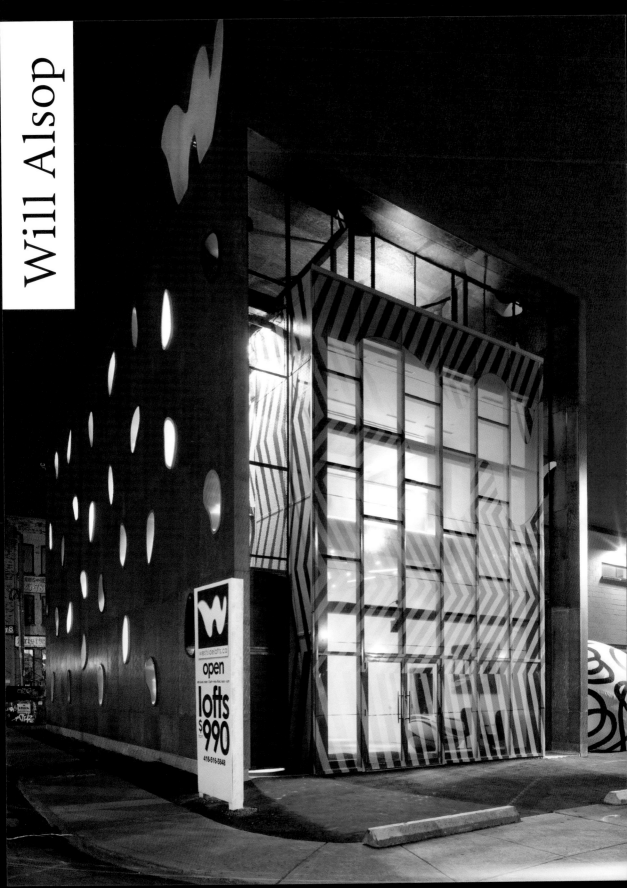

Will Alsop

Westside Sales Center

This pavilion of artistic sculptural quality will one day house a museum. Will Alsop, who has already designed spectacular architecture in Toronto, has now created an object in a small format that serves the lively development activities of the city. Westside is the real-estate center of Toronto today. The mobile building consists of a core of fiber-reinforced concrete panels with sidings of bright red wood and the famous, colorful Alsop Swiss cheese holes as window openings. Snuggled alongside is a white, walk-in sphere for use as office space.

Westside Sales Center

Dieser Pavillon von hoher skulpturaler Qualität wird einmal ein Museum sein. Will Alsop, der in Toronto bereits spektakuläre Architektur baute, hat nun in kleinem Format ein Objekt entworfen, das den regen Entwicklungs- und Erschließungsaktivitäten der Stadt dient. Vorerst befindet sich hier das Immobilienverkaufszentrum Toronto Westside. Das mobile Gebäude besteht aus einem Kern aus Betonfaserplatten, der in leuchtend rotes Holz gekleidet ist und als Fensteröffnungen die berühmten, knallbunten Alsop-Schweizer-Käse-Löcher aufweist. Daneben duckt sich ein weißer, begehbarer Ballon als Büroeinheit.

Bureau de vente de Westside

Ce pavillon à l'esthétique sculpturale sera un jour un musée. Will Alsop, qui a déjà construit d'autres bâtiments spectaculaires à Toronto, a créé ici un objet au format plus réduit, qui sert les activités bouillonnantes de développement et de valorisation de la ville. Pour le moment, Westside est le centre de l'immobilier à Toronto. Ce bâtiment mobile est composé d'un noyau en plaques de béton de fibres revêtu de panneaux en bois rouge intense, et est doté des fameuses fenêtres multicolores en trous de gruyère d'Alsop. La sphère blanche qui se blottit contre le bâtiment est un bureau.

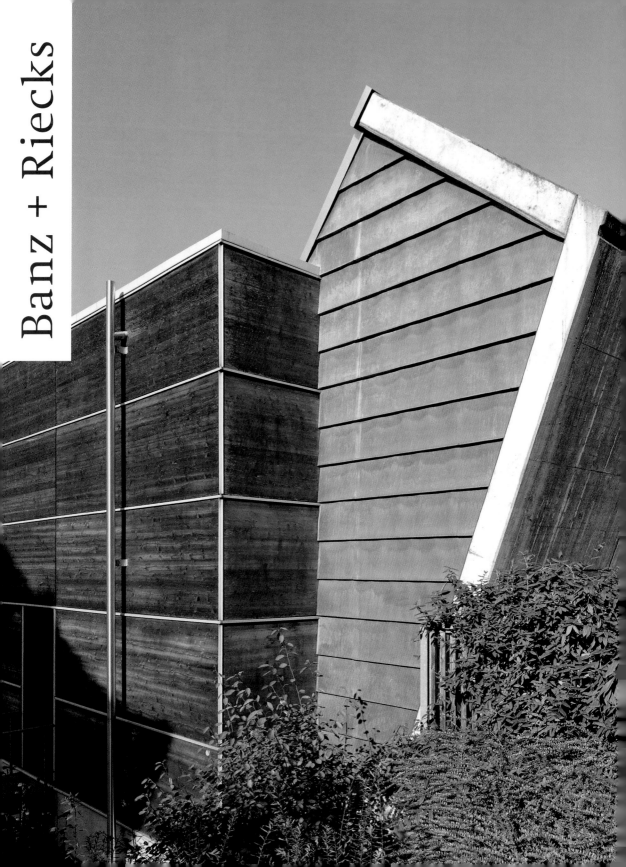

Banz + Riecks

MANNUS Production Room

This production room belonging to a maker of flagpoles has won numerous prizes for its architecture. Not only was the ecologically outstanding energy efficiency recognized, but also the cleverly thought-out functionality of the building, which specifically facilitates the production work. A central request of the client, who had his entire corporate property designed as an exhibition park, was the building's beauty. The building's supporting and surrounding structures are made almost entirely of wood. The natural color and structure of the exterior larch wood siding characterizes the appearance. The single obviously formal and materially outstanding element is the so-called 'light shovel' – a protruding diagonal wall of concrete with a skylight. Spotlights emphasize this wall even more when it is dark.

MANNUS Fertigungshalle

Diese Produktionshalle eines Herstellers von Fahnenmasten ist mehrfach preisgekrönt. Gewürdigt wurde nicht nur das ökologisch herausragende Niedrigenergiekonzept, sondern auch die ausgeklügelte Funktionalität des Gebäudes, die die Produktherstellung gezielt unterstützt. Ein zentrales Anliegen des Auftraggebers, der sein gesamtes Firmengelände als Ausstellungspark gestalten ließ, war gleichwohl die Schönheit des Objektes. Der Bau besteht in seinen konstruktiven und umhüllenden Teilen fast vollständig aus Holz. Die natürliche Färbung und Struktur der Außenverkleidung aus Lärchenholztafeln bestimmt das Bild. Deutlich formal und materiell abgehoben wurde einzig die „Lichtschaufel" – eine ausladende Schrägwand aus Beton mit Oberlicht. Sie wird bei Dunkelheit durch Strahler zusätzlich betont.

Salle de production MANNUS

Cette salle de production où l'on fabrique des mâts de drapeaux a remporté de nombreux prix d'architecture, non seulement pour l'excellence écologique de son concept d'efficience énergétique, mais également pour la réflexion menée sur la fonctionnalité du bâtiment, qui vise à faciliter les activités de production. L'une des requêtes centrales du client, qui a fait concevoir tout le complexe de l'entreprise comme un parc d'exposition, concernait la beauté du bâtiment. L'ossature et le revêtement du bâtiment sont presque entièrement en bois, et son allure est déterminée par la couleur naturelle et la structure du revêtement extérieur en panneaux de mélèze. Le seul élément qui tranche nettement sur les plans formel et matériel est la « pale de lumière », un mur de béton qui fait saillie en diagonale, doté d'une claire-voie. De nuit, des spots mettent ce mur encore plus en valeur.

Two-layer wooden walls provide excellent insulation for the building. Compressed wood and Kerto®-Qpressboard were used in the interior and on the ceiling.

Zweischalige Holzwände gewährleisten eine hervorragende Isolierung des Gebäudes. Innen und an der Decke wurden Pressholz- und Kerto®-Q-Holzplatten verwendet.

Des murs qui abritent une couche isolante entre deux couches de bois dotent le bâtiment d'une excellente isolation. Pour les plafonds, à l'intérieur, on a utilisé du bois comprimé et des panneaux de bois Kerto®-Q.

The depressed windows show the building numbers; shiny metal flagpoles break up the wooden facade.

Die bedruckten Fenster tragen die Numerierung der Werkstore; metallglänzende Fahnenmasten gliedern die Holzfassade.

Les fenêtres imprimées portent les numéros des ateliers, et des mâts métalliques rutilants rythment la façade en bois.

Berger + Parkkinen

The Embassies of the Nordic Countries

The embassies of the Scandinavian countries in Berlin are gathered in a single area adjacent to the zoo grounds. Renowned architectural firms from the respective countries designed the missions of the individual delegations. Berger + Parkkinen created the design concept for the entire 'Nordic Embassies' area, to which the 'Felleshus' Pan Nordic building also belongs.

A striking characteristic of this building is the use of maple on the main facade and for all the interior fittings and furnishings. Because 'Felleshus' functions as an access building for all the embassies, its facade serves as an entrance to the Nordic countries. The building receives visitors with a wall structure of horizontal maple slats that flank the ceiling-height glassed-in entrance.

Die Botschaften der Nordischen Länder

Die skandinavischen Ländervertretungen versammeln sich in Berlin auf einem gemeinsamen Areal, direkt neben dem Tiergartenpark. Die einzelnen Botschaften wurden von renommierten Architekturbüros der jeweiligen Nationen entworfen. Das Atelier Berger + Parkkinen schuf ein Gestaltungskonzept für den Gesamtbereich „Nordische Botschaften", zu dem auch das „Felleshus"-Gemeinschaftshaus gehört.

Ein auffallendes Kennzeichen dieses Gebäudes ist die Verwendung von Ahornholz an der Hauptfassade und in der gesamten Innenausstattung und Möblierung. Da das Felleshus als Zugangsgebäude zu allen Botschaften fungiert, bildet seine Fassade sozusagen das Entree der Nordischen Länder. Mit einer Wandgliederung aus horizontalen Ahornlamellen, die den haushoch verglasten Eingang flankieren, empfängt das Bauwerk den Besucher.

Les ambassades des pays nordiques

Les ambassades des pays nordiques à Berlin sont rassemblées sur un seul terrain, juste à côté du zoo. Des cabinets d'architectes renommés originaires de chaque pays concerné se sont chargés des différentes délégations. L'Atelier Berger + Parkkinen a créé le concept d'ensemble du complexe « Ambassades nordiques », dont fait également partie le centre communautaire « Felleshus ».

L'une de ses caractéristiques les plus frappantes est qu'on y a utilisé de l'érable pour la façade principale ainsi que pour tous les aménagements intérieurs et pour le mobilier. Le Felleshus étant le passage qui mène à toutes les ambassades, sa façade est en quelque sorte une porte d'entrée vers les pays nordiques. Les visiteurs y sont accueillis par ses murs en lattes d'érable horizontales qui flanquent l'entrée vitrée sur toute la hauteur du bâtiment.

The embassy buildings stand near each other as if in a small village and create architecturally stimulating neighborhoods: here you can see the wood facade of the Finnish mission.

Wie in einem kleinen Dorf stehen die Botschaftsgebäude beieinander und bilden architektonisch reizvolle Nachbarschaften: hier blickt man auf eine Holzfassade der finnischen Vertretung.

Les ambassades se dressent côte à côte, comme dans un petit village, et créent un paysage architectural plein de charme : on voit ici la façade en bois de la délégation finlandaise.

The striped shape of the Felleshus windows softens the entering daylight. Grayish-white exposed concrete together with the maple's soft grain give the interior a friendly feel.

Durch die streifenförmigen Fenster des Felleshus fällt gedämpftes Tageslicht ein. Weißgrauer Sichtbeton verleiht gemeinsam mit dem zart gemaserten Ahornholz den Innenräumen einen freundlichen Charakter.

Les panneaux horizontaux des fenêtres du Felleshus tamisent la lumière du jour. Le béton brut gris-blanc et la texture délicate de l'érable confèrent à l'intérieur une atmosphère chaleureuse.

The cafeteria serves Nordic specialties.

In der Kantine werden nordische Spezialitäten serviert.

La cafétéria sert des spécialités nordiques.

Klaus Block

Library in the Church

St. Mary's city parish church in Müncheberg (Germany) is unusual for its multifunctional uses – as a place of worship, city library and cultural center – whose motto is "Ruins Under a Roof." Also unusual is the versatility of its architecture. The remains of different historical buildings, including a gothic Cistercian church and an F. K. Schinkel classical renovation, were reconstructed while keeping their fragmented character as separate rooms. Professor Klaus Block placed the library here as a freestanding unit whose shape is much like a ship's bilge – the feeling is similar to a church's nave. This structure paneled in ash wood slats is accessible by way of several landings at different heights. Views both into and out of the library are made possible by the light covering.

Bibliothek in der Kirche

Ungewöhnlich ist die Multifunktionalität der Stadtpfarrkirche St. Marien in Müncheberg, die unter dem Motto „Ruine unter Dach" als Gottesdienstraum, Stadtbibliothek und Kulturzentrum genutzt wird. Ungewöhnlich ist auch die Architektur in ihrer Vielschichtigkeit. Die Überreste verschiedener historischer Vorgängerbauten – darunter eine gotische Zisterzienserkirche und ein klassizistischer Umbau von F. K. Schinkel – waren als bewusst fragmenthafter Raum wiedererrichtet worden. Dort hinein setzte Prof. Klaus Block die Bibliothek als einen freistehenden Körper, der in etwa die Form eines Schiffsbauches hat – man fühlt sich an den Begriff des Kirchenschiffes erinnert. Über Stege auf unterschiedlicher Höhe ist dieser mit Eschenholzlamellen verkleidete Einbau zugänglich. Wechselseitige Durchblicke aus der und in die Bibliothek sind durch die lichte Ummantelung möglich.

Bibliothèque dans l'église

L'église paroissiale Sainte-Marie de Müncheberg (Allemagne), dont la devise est « des ruines sous un toit » se distingue par sa multifonctionnalité : c'est un lieu de culte, une bibliothèque municipale et un centre culturel. La diversité de son architecture est également assez inhabituelle. Les vestiges de plusieurs bâtiments historiques (dont une église gothique cistercienne et une rénovation classique de F. K. Schinkel) ont été reconstruits pour former des pièces fragmentées. Le professeur Klaus Block a fait de la bibliothèque un volume isolé en forme de coque de bateau, qui évoque la nef d'une église. On accède à cette structure revêtue de lattes de frêne par plusieurs passerelles installées à différentes hauteurs. La légèreté du revêtement permet un échange visuel entre la bibliothèque et l'extérieur.

The library consists of three stories accessible via a free-standing elevator tower.

Die Bibliothek umfasst drei Etagen, die über einen frei stehenden Aufzugsturm erreichbar sind.

Une tour d'ascenseur isolée donne accès aux trois étages de la bibliothèque.

Its translucent wood walls relieve the building of any heaviness and let brightness from the church windows stream inside.

Seine lichtdurchlässigen Holz-wände nehmen dem Einbau die Schwere und lassen Helligkeit von den Kirchenfenstern bis in den Innenraum vordringen

Ses murs ajourés en bois évitent toute lourdeur et laissent pénétrer la lumière des fenêtres de l'église.

Bonte & Migozzi

Beach Rescue Station

The specialists in wood architecture and ecologically sound building have once again found an aesthetic solution for a functional structure. It was important to the architects to unobtrusively integrate the rescue station into the coastal landscape of Marseille beach. As a result, the buildings were kept as far as possible from the water, pressing themselves flat into the dunes and open on all sides. The vertical wood grid of the walls is stationary, but the spaces between the slats are situated to produce the ideal balance of sunlight and shade. They allow enough of a view that no real windows are needed. The rectangular openings on the front of the building allow for greater interaction with the public. The materials were selected for their limited environmental impact, imposing appearance and a color palette that harmonizes with the surroundings: European conifer wood, along with tin and copper for the roofs.

Strand-Rettungsposten

Die Spezialisten für Holzarchitektur und ökologisches Bauen haben erneut eine ästhetische Lösung für einen Zweckbau gefunden. Die sanfte Integrierung der Rettungsstation in das Küstenlandschaftsbild am Strand von Marseille war den Architekten wichtig. Deshalb wurden die Gebäude auf größtmögliche Distanz zum Wasser gehalten, ducken sich flach in die Dünen und öffnen sich doch nach allen Seiten. Das vertikale Holzraster der Wände ist nicht beweglich, die Leistenzwischenräume sind aber so berechnet, dass sie den idealen Ausgleich von Sonneneinstrahlung und Schatten erzeugen. Sie ermöglichen genügend Durchblicke, so dass keine echten Fenster benötigt wurden. Die querrechteckigen Luken in den Vorderseiten der Gebäude dienen mehr der Interaktion mit dem Publikum. Die Materialien wurden im Hinblick auf Umweltverträglichkeit, edle Ausstrahlung und farbliche Harmonie mit der Umgebung ausgewählt: europäische Nadelhölzer, sowie Zinn und Kupfer für die Dächer.

Poste de secours sur la plage

Les spécialistes de l'architecture écologique en bois ont encore une fois trouvé une solution esthétique pour un bâtiment fonctionnel. Pour les architectes, il était important d'intégrer le poste de secours au paysage côtier de la plage marseillaise en toute discrétion: les bâtiments ont été construits aussi loin que possible de l'eau, ils se pressent à plat contre les dunes et s'ouvrent sur tous les côtés. La grille verticale des murs en bois est fixe, mais les lattes sont espacées de façon à créer un équilibre idéal entre ombre et soleil. Elles donnent une visibilité suffisante pour éliminer le besoin de véritables fenêtres. Les ouvertures rectangulaires percées sur l'avant du bâtiment favorisent l'interaction avec le public. Les matériaux ont été sélectionnés en fonction de leur impact sur l'environnement, de leurs qualités esthétiques et de leur couleur, qui se fond dans le paysage : du bois de conifère européen, et de l'étain et du cuivre pour le toit.

Nothing here calls to mind the unsightly temporary arrangements where lifeguards are housed on so many coasts.

Nichts erinnert hier an die unansehnlichen Provisorien, in denen an vielen Küsten die Rettungswachten untergebracht sind.

Rien ici ne rappelle les structures temporaires inesthétiques que les maîtres nageurs occupent habituellement sur les plages.

The graphical concepts on the signs and the color palette of the interior fittings were designed as part of a cohesive whole.

Auch das grafische Konzept der Hinweisschilder und das Farbdesign der Inneneinrichtung haben eine konsequente Gestaltung erfahren.

Les concepts graphiques des panneaux et la palette de couleur de l'aménagement intérieur ont été conçus pour s'inscrire dans un ensemble cohérent.

Gianni Botsford Architects

Casa Kike

Casa Kike was built in Costa Rica as a heavenly estate for a writer and his library of nearly 20,000 titles. Bookshelves occupy all wall spaces in the house's interior, while organizing it and bringing it to life. Right angles were shunned throughout in favor of expressive diagonals. This is apparent in the spaces between the beams of the timber-frame construction, in the ceiling timbers and in the exterior building form. A wooden pavilion is completely reserved for the books, a desk and a grand piano. The building's twin that houses the living and sleeping areas is accessible via a breezeway. The avant-garde architecture is influenced by the local building technique: it rests on stilts, as is the norm here, and is made of the termite- and waterproof Cacha hardwood. Procurement of this material in this country is extremely time-consuming due to strict environmental-protection controls. Large areas of Costa Rica are nature preserves.

Casa Kike

Casa Kike wurde als paradiesisches Anwesen für einen Schriftsteller mit seiner knapp 20.000 Buchexemplare umfassenden Bibliothek in Costa Rica erbaut. Bücherregale nehmen alle Wandflächen innerhalb des Hauses ein, gliedern und beleben diese. Rechte Winkel wurden immer wieder zugunsten expressiver Schrägen verbannt. Dies zeigt sich in den Gefachen, im Dachgebälk und in der äußeren Gebäudeform. Ein Holzpavillon ist ganz den Büchern, einem Schreibtisch und einem Flügel vorbehalten. Über einen Steg gelangt man zu einem Zwillingsgebäude mit Wohn- und Schlafräumen. Die avantgardistische Architektur ist beeinflusst von der lokalen Bauweise: Sie ruht auf Stelzen, wie hier üblich, und besteht aus Cachàholz, das in seiner Härte termiten- und wasserfest ist. Die Materialbeschaffung ist in diesem Land wegen äußerst strenger Umweltschutzauflagen sehr zeitraubend. Weite Teile Costa Ricas sind Naturschutzgebiet.

Casa Kike

Casa Kike est une résidence paradisiaque construite en Costa Rica pour loger un écrivain et sa bibliothèque de près de 20 000 titres. À l'intérieur, tous les murs sont occupés par des étagères remplies de livres qui organisent l'espace et lui donnent vie. Les angles droits ont été bannis partout en faveur de diagonales expressives. Cette caractéristique est bien visible dans les croisillons, dans la charpente et dans la forme extérieure de la maison. Un pavillon en bois est réservé exclusivement aux livres, à un bureau et à un piano à queue. Une passerelle mène à un autre pavillon, identique, qui abrite les espaces de vie et les chambres. L'architecture avant-gardiste est influencée par une technique de construction locale : le bâtiment repose sur des pilotis, ce qui est la norme dans la région, et est construit en bois de Cachà, qui résiste aux termites et à l'eau. Dans ce pays, il faut beaucoup de temps pour se procurer ce matériau, car il est régi par des contrôles de protection de l'environnement très stricts. De larges étendues du Costa Rica sont des réserves naturelles.

This rare hardwood is so dense it sinks in water.

Das seltene Hartholz hat eine so hohe Dichte, dass es in Wasser sinkt.

Ce bois dur rare est tellement dense qu'il coule dans l'eau.

The end walls of the pavilion are covered in glass. The windows function as vents; their open glass slats allow adequate ventilation in the library.

Die Stirnseiten der Pavillons sind ganz verglast. Die Fenster funktionieren wie Jalousien; ihre geöffneten Glaslamellen sorgen für eine ausreichende Belüftung der Bibliothek.

Les façades du pavillon sont revêtues de verre. Les fenêtres fonctionnent comme des stores : leurs lames de verre ouvertes donnent à la bibliothèque une aération suffisante.

Gion A. Caminada

Stiva da Morts (Memorial Room)

Internationally renowned architect Gion A. Caminada constantly incorporates locally proven building techniques in his projects. In his hometown of Vrin (Switzerland), he contributes to the preservation and revitalization of social processes through his buildings, and, as a result, helps counter the threatening population drain. He had absolutely no reservations about the idea of a memorial room for this location. It serves as a public mourning hall for the whole community, but its dimensions and floor plan are reminiscent of traditional memorial services in farmhouses. It lies on a slope below the church, has entrances and exits on two floors and seems much like a small private home, with different rooms that host particular parts of the memorial service (living room, kitchen and hallway). The wooden building's material and construction are in line with local buildings, and it was built as a so-called 'double Strickbau.'

Stiva da Morts (Totenstube)

Der international renommierte Architekt Gion A. Caminada setzt sich in seinen Projekten immer wieder für die Erhaltung bewährter lokaler Bautraditionen ein. In seinem Heimatort Vrin (Schweiz) trägt er mit seinen Bauten zur Erhaltung und Wiederbelebung gesellschaftlicher Prozesse bei und hilft damit, der drohenden Bevölkerungsabwanderung entgegen zu wirken. Keinerlei Berührungsängste hatte er mit der Konzipierung einer Totenstube für den Ort. Sie dient als öffentliche Trauerhalle für die ganze Gemeinde, ist jedoch in ihren Dimensionen und ihrer räumlichen Struktur dem herkömmlichen Totengedächtnis in den Bauernhäusern nachempfunden. Sie liegt am Hang unterhalb der Kirche, hat auf zwei Etagen Ein- und Ausgänge und wirkt wie ein kleines Privathaus mit verschiedenen Räumlichkeiten, die bestimmte Abschnitte im Trauerritual aufnehmen (Stube, Küche, Gang). Das Holzgebäude entspricht in Material und Konstruktion der einheimischen Bebauung und wurde als sogenannter doppelter Strickbau errichtet.

Stiva da Morts (chambre funéraire)

Gion A. Caminada est un architecte au renom international, qui intègre toujours à ses projets des techniques de construction locales. Dans sa ville natale de Vrin, en Suisse, il contribue à la préservation et à la dynamisation des processus sociaux grâce à ses bâtiments, et aide ainsi à contrer la menace de l'exode de la population. L'idée d'une chambre funéraire pour ce lieu ne lui a posé absolument aucun problème. Elle sert de funérarium public pour toute la communauté, mais ses dimensions et son agencement évoquent les services funéraires traditionnels des fermes. Elle se dresse sur une pente sous l'église, est dotée d'entrées et de sorties sur deux étages et ressemble beaucoup à une petite maison privée dont les différentes pièces accueilleraient les différentes parties du service funéraire (salon, cuisine, vestibule). Ce bâtiment en bois s'intègre à l'architecture locale par ses matériaux et sa construction, et a été érigé dans le style « double Strickbau », avec des madriers carrés.

The Casein paint matt white exterior of this wooden building creates a visual relationship with the facade of the neighboring church.

Die mit Kaseinfarbe mattweiß geschlemmte Außenseite des Holzbaus stellt einen optischen Bezug zur Fassade der benachbarten Kirche her.

L'extérieur peint en blanc laiteux mat établit un lien visuel avec la façade de l'église voisine.

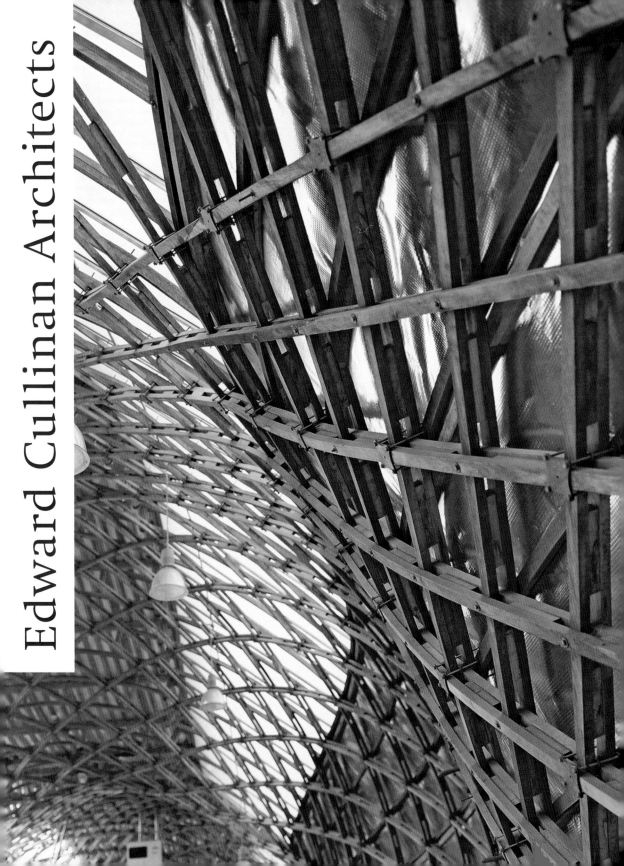

Edward Cullinan Architects

Weald & Downland Museum

Weald & Downland is one of Great Britain's largest open-air museums. At least 40 historical buildings were removed from locations around the country, rebuilt here and restored to their original specifications. Edward Cullinan Architects created a new building with an unusual form to accommodate the preservation work, display areas and visitor education space, which harmonizes with the landscape and fits in with the old buildings. A parabola-shaped domed ceiling curves up at double the height of the half-height semi-basement. The roof forms three waves on the long axis and resembles a hilly landscape. Bands of small windows along the roof ridge brighten the interior. The roof vault consists of an oak grid whose artistic craftsmanship and aesthetic appeal captivate the visitor. Outside, the roof is covered with strips of red cedar arranged in three long rows that accentuate the extended wave-like shape of the roof.

Weald & Downland Museum

Weald & Downland ist eines der größten Freilichtmuseen Großbritanniens. Gut 40 historische Gebäude wurden an verschiedenen Orten des Landes abgetragen, hier wiederaufgebaut und originalgetreu restauriert. Für die konservatorische Arbeit, Ausstellungszwecke und Besucherkurse entwarf das Büro Edward Cullinan Architects einen Neubau von ungewöhnlicher Form, der sich dennoch harmonisch in das Gelände und zwischen die alten Gebäude einfügt. Über ein halbhohes Sockelgeschoss wölbt sich ein gut doppelt so hohes Kuppeldach mit parabelförmigem Schnitt. In der Längsrichtung bildet das Dach drei Wellen und erinnert an eine Hügellandschaft. Lichtbänder beidseits des Firstes beleuchten das Innere. Das Dachgewölbe besteht aus einem Eichenholzgitter dessen handwerkliche Kunstfertigkeit und großer ästhetischer Reiz den Besucher in den Bann ziehen. Außen ist das Dach mit Rotzedernleisten verkleidet, die in drei langen Bahnen verlegt wurden und so die lang gestreckte Wellenlinie des Daches betonen.

Musée Weald & Downland

Weald & Downland est l'un des plus grands musées de plein air en Grande-Bretagne. Une quarantaine de bâtiments historiques ont été prélevés à travers tout le pays, et ont été reconstruits et restaurés selon leurs conditions d'origine. Le cabinet d'architectes Edward Cullinan a créé un nouveau bâtiment à la forme inhabituelle pour accueillir les activités de conservation et les espaces d'exposition et d'éducation des visiteurs, en toute harmonie avec le paysage et les bâtiments anciens. Le dôme parabolique de la toiture s'arrondit au double de la hauteur du demi-étage de la base. Il forme trois ondulations en longueur sur son axe et évoque un paysage vallonné. L'intérieur est éclairé par deux bandes de fenêtres situées de part et d'autre du faîte. La voûte de la toiture est formée d'une grille en chêne dont le travail artistique et la beauté captivent les visiteurs. À l'extérieur, le toit est couvert de planches de cèdre rouge posées en trois longues rangées qui soulignent son ondulation.

This building won the European Wooden Facade Award in 2004.

Das Gebäude erhielt 2004 den European Wooden Façade Award.

Ce bâtiment a été récompensé par le prix European Wooden Façade en 2004.

The superior carpentry was completed entirely by artisans from the region.

Die anspruchsvollen Zimmermannsarbeiten wurden ausschließlich von Handwerkern der Region ausgeführt.

La charpente remarquable est entièrement l'œuvre d'artisans de la région.

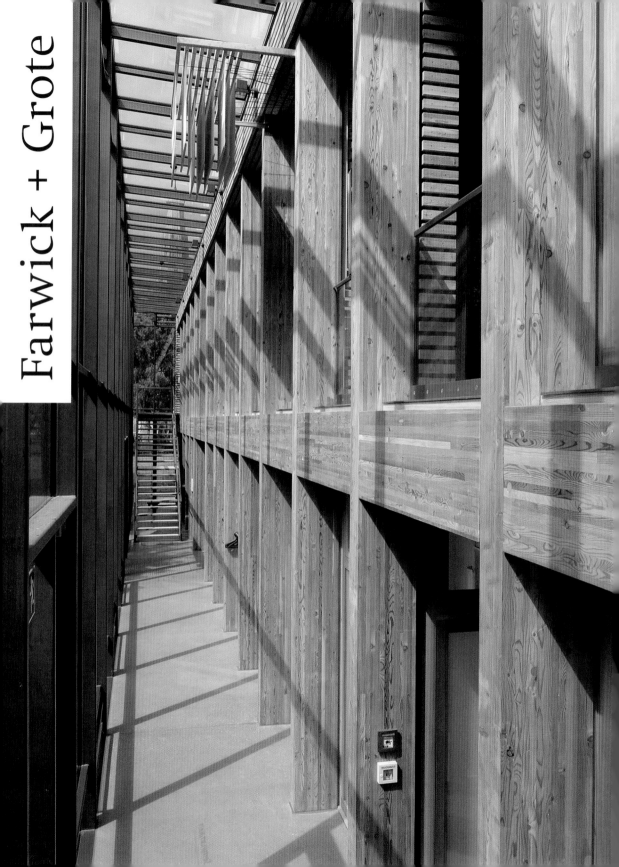

Information Center Raesfeld Castle and Zoo

Wooden facades behind glass are a subject of modern wood architecture. Wood becomes a fine, decorative element and glass performs a protective function, analogous to a china cabinet that showcases its precious contents. Such is the idea by Farwick + Grote Architects. In addition, the surrounding park reflects in the smooth outer skin and the space between the larch wall and glass is accessible. The freestanding, simple solitary building houses an information center for the castle and zoo and is also used as a city cultural and educational forum.

Informationszentrum Tiergarten Schloss Raesfeld

Holzfassaden hinter Glas sind ein neues Thema moderner Holzarchitektur. Holz wird zum edlen, dekorativen Element und Glas übernimmt eine schützende Funktion, die in Analogie zur Vitrine den edlen Inhalt noch hervorhebt. So will auch das Konzept von Farwick + Grote Architekten verstanden werden. Zudem spiegelt sich in der glatten Außenhaut die Parkumgebung, der Raum zwischen Lärchenholzwand und Glas ist begehbar. Der freistehende, schlichte Gebäudesolitär beherbergt ein Informationszentrum zu Schloss und Tierpark und wird als städtisches Kultur- und Bildungsforum genutzt.

Centre d'information du zoo du château de Raesfeld

Les façades en bois abritées derrière du verre sont un sujet d'actualité dans l'architecture en bois. Le bois devient un élément décoratif noble et le verre adopte une fonction de protection, analogue à celle d'une vitrine qui met en valeur son précieux contenu. C'est ainsi qu'il faut appréhender le concept des architectes de Farwick + Grote. Le parc environnant se reflète en outre sur le revêtement lisse et l'on peut déambuler dans l'espace entre le verre et le mur en mélèze. Ce bâtiment simple et isolé abrite un centre d'information rattaché au château et au zoo, et est également un forum culturel et pédagogique communal.

The large main room can be configured for various types of events and remains flooded with light regardless of configuration.

Der große Hauptraum lässt sich für verschiedene Veranstaltungszwecke modifizieren und bleibt dabei stets lichtdurchflutet.

La configuration de la grande salle principale peut être modifiée pour accueillir différents types d'événements, mais reste dans tous les cas inondée de lumière.

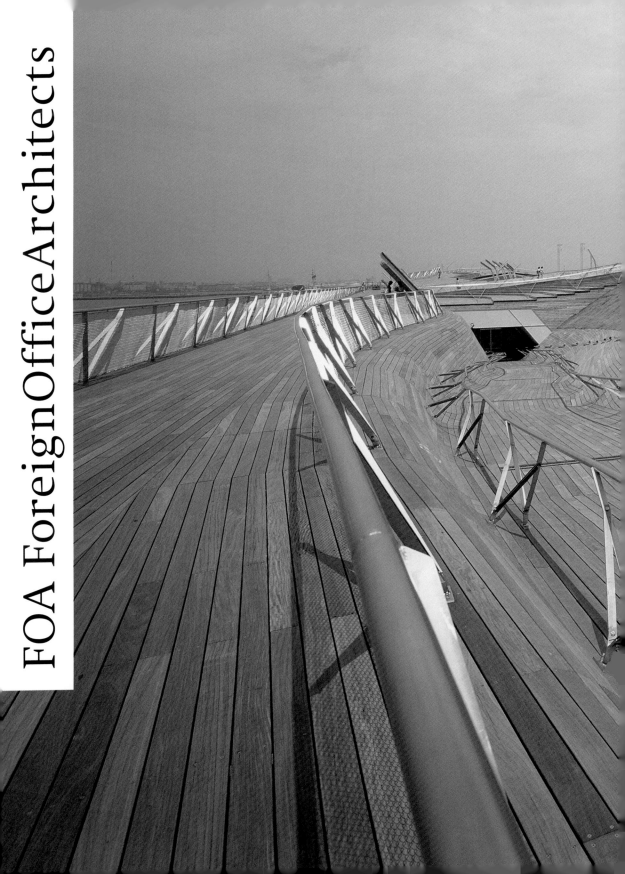

FOA ForeignOfficeArchitects

Harbor Terminal

FOA achieved their definitive breakthrough into world-class architecture with this completely novel and courageous realization of a large-scale building project. The radical approach of completely uncoupling architecture from the fundamental idea of load bearing and surrounding structures proved extremely useful for this project: instead of pillars and walls, there is a fusion of ramps, diagonal supports and dome systems made of diagonals. Visitors move as if through a crystal in this landscape of wood, metal, glass and green spaces. The new pier is not a rigid system of paths, but rather an extension and enlargement of the adjoining neighborhoods. Residents use the area as a park or public square, even when they have nothing to do with passenger shipping. The complicated parquet pattern, complex surface relief and multiple levels arise from narrow, very long wooden planks. Computer-aided design and construction preparations were indispensable for this project.

Hafenterminal

Mit seiner völlig neuartigen und mutigen Realisierung eines Großbauprojektes erreichte FOA den endgültigen Durchbruch in die Weltspitzenarchitektur. Der radikale Ansatz, Architektur vom Grundkonzept der tragenden und umhüllenden Teile zu lösen, erwies sich für diesen Auftrag als sinnvoll: An Stelle von Stütze und Wand findet sich hier eine Durchdringung von Rampen, schrägen Verstrebungen und aus Diagonalen gebildeten Kuppelsystemen. Man bewegt sich wie durch einen Kristall in dieser aus Holz, Metall, Glas und Grünflächen modellierten Landschaft. Der neue Pier ist kein starres Wegesystem, sondern eine Erweiterung und Bereicherung der angrenzenden Stadtgebiete. Die Anwohner nutzen ihn als Park oder öffentlichen Platz, auch wenn sie nicht mit dem Personenschiffsverkehr in Berührung kommen. Aus sehr langen Holzplanken wurde das komplizierte Parkettmuster, das komplexe Oberflächenrelief und mehrere Raumschichten erzeugt. Die computergestützte Konstruktionsvorbereitung war dabei unabdingbar.

Terminal portuaire

Avec la réalisation audacieuse et innovatrice de ce projet à grande échelle, FOA a définitivement percé dans le domaine de l'architecture internationale. La démarche radicale que le cabinet a adoptée, consistant à désolidariser l'architecture des concepts de base de structures porteuses et d'habillage, s'est révélée très judicieuse pour ce projet : au lieu de piliers et de murs, on trouve ici une combinaison de rampes, de supports obliques et de systèmes de dômes composés de diagonales. Dans ce paysage de bois, de métal, de verre et d'espaces verts, le visiteur déambule dans un cristal. Le nouvel embarcadère n'est pas un système rigide d'itinéraires, il s'agit plutôt d'un prolongement des quartiers voisins. Les riverains utilisent cet espace comme un parc ou une place publique, même lorsque leurs activités n'ont rien à voir avec le transport de passagers. De longues et minces planches de bois donnent naissance au motif compliqué du parquet, aux reliefs de la surface et aux multiples niveaux. La conception assistée par ordinateur s'est révélée indispensable pour préparer le chantier.

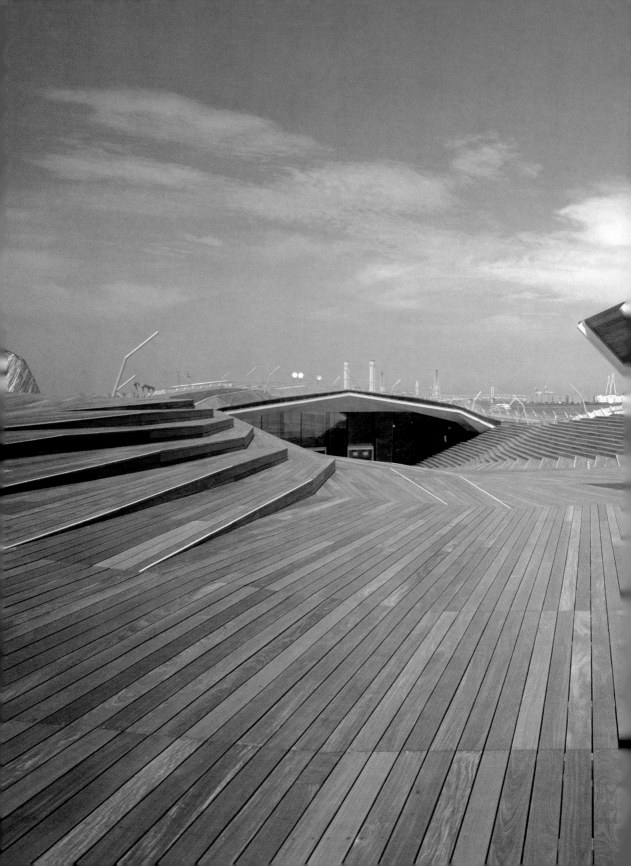

The pier's landscape invites walks.

Die Landschaft des Piers lädt zum Spaziergang ein.

Le paysage de l'embarcadère invite à la promenade.

Right angles are absent from the architecture, the details of the railings and the awnings.

Rechte Winkel findet man weder in der Architektur noch in den Details der Geländer oder Sonnendächer.

On ne trouve aucun angle droit dans l'architecture, dans le terrain ou dans les auvents.

Gassner & Zarecky

Pfeiffer House

Gassner & Zarecky built four individual structures on the forest edge of a southern German housing development – each a unique variation on the theme of a wooden house. Wood is generally a preferred building material of architects and was to play a special role in the relationship to the surroundings in this case. All of the houses are wood-frame constructions. Pfeiffer House shows an irregular relief of raw boards on the top half of the wall facing the forest. These were placed horizontally in the facade with the bark side facing out. In contrast, the interior rooms and their many built-ins – including floor and ceiling – are entirely made of smooth wood boards. A musician lives in this property, which is why the acoustic qualities were a main reason for using wood.

Haus Pfeiffer

Am Waldrand einer Einfamilienhaussiedlung in Süddeutschland bauten Gassner & Zarecky vier individuelle Objekte – jedes eine ganz eigentümliche Variation des Themas Holzhaus. Holz ist generell ein bevorzugtes Material der Architekten und sollte in diesem Fall auf besondere Weise in Bezug zur natürlichen Umgebung gesetzt werden. Alle Häuser sind in Holzständerbauweise errichtet. Haus Pfeiffer zeigt zur Waldseite hin in der oberen Wandhälfte ein unregelmäßiges Relief aus sägerauen Brettern. Diese wurden in horizontaler Anordnung und mit ihrer Baumrindenseite nach außen in die Fassade gesteckt. Einen Kontrast dazu stellen die Innenräume mit ihren zahlreichen Einbauten dar, die vollflächig – einschließlich Boden und Decke – aus glatten Holzplatten erstellt wurden. Die Immobilie wird von einem Musiker bewohnt. Daher waren akustische Qualitäten ein weiteres Argument für die Verwendung von Holz.

Maison Pfeiffer

Le cabinet Gassner & Zarecky a construit quatre structures individuelles à la lisière de la forêt dans un complexe de pavillons résidentiels, dont chacune est une variation unique sur le thème de la maison en bois. Le bois est en général l'un des matériaux de construction préférés des architectes, et devait ici établir une relation particulière avec l'environnement naturel. Toutes les maisons sont dotées d'une charpente en bois. La résidence Pfeiffer présente un relief irrégulier de planches brutes dans la partie supérieure du mur qui fait face à la forêt. Ces planches ont été disposées à l'horizontale, avec l'écorce vers l'extérieur. Elles créent un contraste avec les pièces en bois lisse du sol au plafond, y compris leurs nombreux éléments intégrés. C'est un musicien qui occupe cette maison. Les qualités acoustiques du bois ont donc été un facteur décisif.

The smooth wood finish of the entire interior, including floor, wall, ceiling and built-ins, helps this rather small floor plan give a generous impression of space.

Die glatte Holzhaut des gesamten Interieurs, einschließlich Boden, Wand, Decke und Einbauten, bewirkt auch auf diesem eher kleinen Grundriss einen großzügigen Raumeindruck.

La finition très lisse du bois dans tout l'intérieur, y compris les sols, les murs, les plafonds et les éléments intégrés, contribue à donner une sensation d'espace généreux dans cette construction aux dimensions plutôt modestes.

The wood paneling was combined with shadow gap technique.

Die Holzverkleidung wurde mit dem Gestaltungsmittel der Schattenfuge kombiniert.

Le revêtement en panneaux de bois a été combiné à la technique du joint creux fermé.

Kellner House

Kellner House exhibits two further variations on the wooden facade. The entire southeast side is a layer of stacked irregular pieces of wood, whereby the raw ends of wood create the pattern that can be seen from the exterior. An external glass wall protects and holds this wall of cut wood pieces, presenting the wood behind the glass as in a showcase. In addition, a glass and wood wall becomes a temperature-regulating solar energy reservoir.
The other side of the house is affixed with a shell of wooden slats. Portions of this siding are movable and open as sliding shutters. When the shutters are closed, it is impossible from the outside to know where the windows are located. Nevertheless, plenty of soft light streams through the spaces between the slats to the interior.

Haus Kellner

Haus Kellner zeigt zwei weitere Spielarten einer Holzfassade. Der gesamten Südostseite ist eine Schicht aus gestapelten Holzscheiten vorgeblendet, wobei man von außen auf das Muster schaut, welches sich aus den Schnittflächen der Scheite ergibt. Diese Scheitewand wird von einer äußeren Glaswand geschützt und gehalten – das dahinter liegende Material wird wie in einem Schaufenster präsentiert. Eine Glas-Holz-Wand ist zudem ein wärmeausgleichender Sonnenenergiespeicher.
Auf den anderen Seiten des Hauses wurde eine Holzleistenschalung angebracht. Einzelne Abschnitte dieser Verkleidung sind beweglich und als Schiebeläden zu öffnen. Bei geschlossenen Läden erkennt man von außen nicht, wo sich Fenster befinden. Nach innen gelangt jedoch durch die Leistenzwischenräume auch dann noch genügend gedämpftes Licht.

Maison Kellner

La maison Kellner présente deux autres variations sur le thème de la façade en bois. Tout le côté sud-est est formé d'une couche de bûchettes irrégulières empilées dont les extrémités composent le motif que l'on voit de l'extérieur. Une paroi de verre protège et maintient ce mur de bûches, et fonctionne comme une vitrine qui présente le bois. Ce mur en verre et en bois fait en outre office de réservoir d'énergie solaire et régule la température.
L'autre côté de la maison est habillé d'un coffrage en lattes de bois doté de parties mobiles qui s'ouvrent comme des volets coulissants. De l'extérieur, lorsque les volets sont fermés, on ne peut pas savoir où se trouvent les fenêtres. Les espaces entre les lattes laissent cependant pénétrer une abondante lumière tamisée.

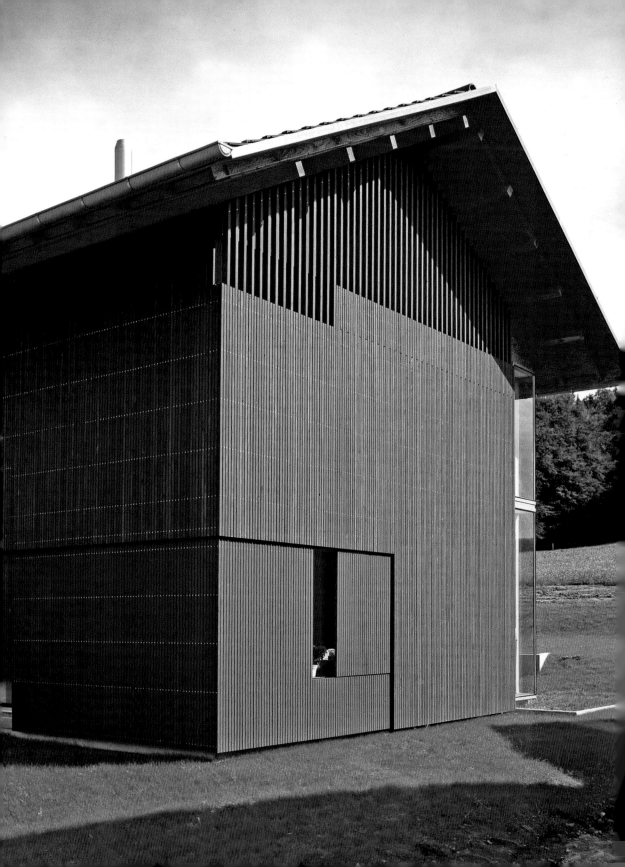

Asymmetry relieves the severity
of the siding.

Asymetrien lockern die Strenge
der Holzleistenverkleidung auf.

Les asymétries compensent
l'austérité de ce revêtement en
bois.

One almost expects the woodpiles
at the southeast side to be carried
away in winter, slowly revealing
the living rooms behind.

Fast erwartet man, dass die
Holzstapel im Winter abgetragen
werden und dahinter allmählich
die Wohnräume zum Vorschein
kommen.

L'on s'attend presque à ce que les
bûches soient utilisées en hiver, et
disparaissent peu à peu pour
révéler les pièces qu'elles cachent.

Serpentine Gallery Pavilion

The Serpentine Gallery Pavilions boast both avant-garde and established architectural firms among their creators. All appeared to feel liberated by the task of creating an ephemeral structure to host the art gallery's summer activities. The strong construction of Frank O. Gehry and his son Samuel Gehry appears experimental and sketchy, like an architecture model or sculpture. At the same time, the father reaches down to his architectural roots: deconstructivism and ecologically friendly building. The Pavilion is Frank O. Gehry's first architectural work in England.

Serpentine Gallery Pavillon

Avantgardisten und etablierte Architekturbüros finden sich gleichermaßen unter den Schöpfern der bisher neun Serpentine Gallery Pavillons in London. Alle scheinen von der Aufgabe, eine ephemere Struktur für die Sommeraktivitäten der Kunstgalerie zu schaffen, wie befreit. Die kraftvolle Konstruktion von Frank O. Gehry und Samuel Gehry, seinem Sohn, wirkt experimentell und skizzenhaft wie ein Architekturmodell oder wie eine Skulptur. Gleichzeitig berührt der Vater hier seine architektonischen Wurzeln: den Dekonstruktivismus und das ökologische Bauen. Der Pavillon ist Frank O. Gehrys erste architektonische Arbeit in England.

Pavillon de la Serpentine Gallery

Les neuf pavillons de la Serpentine Gallery comptent aussi bien des cabinets d'architectes avant-gardistes qu'établis de longue date parmi leurs créateurs. Tous semblent se sentir libérés par la création d'une structure éphémère destinée à accueillir les activités estivales de la galerie. La construction puissante de Frank O. Gehry et de son fils Samuel Gehry a une allure expérimentale et graphique, comme une maquette ou une sculpture. Dans le même temps, le père retrouve ses racines architecturales : le déconstructivisme et les constructions écologiques. Ce pavillon est la première œuvre architecturale de Frank O. Gehry en Angleterre.

A path leads from Kensington Gardens Park to the Serpentine Gallery. The Gehrys' Pavilion guards it like a monumental gate.

Ein Weg führt von Kensington Gardens Park zur Serpentine Gallery. Er wird vom Pavillon der Gehrys wie von einem monumentalen Tor überdacht.

Un chemin mène du parc de Kensington Gardens à la Serpentine Gallery. Le pavillon des Gehry y monte la garde tel une porte monumentale.

Participants at events in the park can linger on different levels throughout the construction.

Die Teilnehmer der Veranstaltungen im Park können sich auf verschiedenen Ebenen innerhalb der Konstruktion aufhalten.

Les participants aux événements du parc peuvent s'attarder sur les différents niveaux à l'intérieur de la structure.

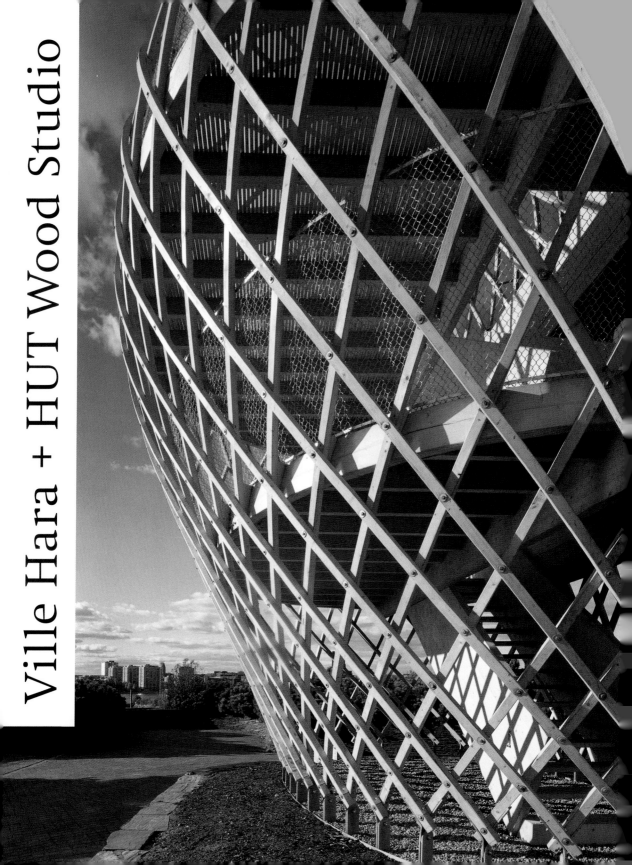

Ville Hara + HUT Wood Studio

Kupla Observation Tower

Helsinki University of Technology plays a central role in the further development of traditional Scandinavian wood architecture. HUT students can apply to the Wood Studio Workshop, where they learn myriad architectural disciplines as they relate to wood. Wood Focus Finland was the 2002 design contest for an observation tower in Helsinki Zoo. Ville Hara, an internationally prolific architect from Finland, designed the winning entry realized in Wood Studio. Using a two-meter tall wooden model, several important architectural decisions were made during prep-work. Ville Hara chose an organic form and built a lattice of laminated bentwood. The tower's high all-around stability functions like an eggshell – if one point is injured, the entire structure remains stable.

Aussichtsturm "Kupla"

Bei der Weiterentwicklung der traditionellen skandinavischen Holzarchitektur nimmt die HUT Helsinki University of Technology eine zentrale Rolle ein. An der Hochschule können sich Studierende um die Teilnahme am Wood Studio Workshop bewerben, in dem rund um das Material Holz verschiedenste Disziplinen der Architektur geschult werden. 2002 wurde mit Wood Focus Finnland ein Wettbewerb für einen Aussichtsturm im Zoo Helsinki ausgelobt. Von Ville Hara, einem heute international tätigen Architekten aus Finnland, stammt der Siegerentwurf, der im Wood Studio realisiert wurde. Bei der Vorbereitung konnten anhand eines 2 m hohen Modells, ebenfalls aus Holz, einige wichtige architektonische Entscheidungen getroffen werden. Ville Hara wählte eine organische Form und konstruierte eine Netzstruktur aus schichtverleimtem Bugholz. Deren hohe allseitige Stabilität funktioniert wie bei einer Eischale – würde ein Punkt verletzt, bliebe die Statik der Gesamtform dennoch gewährleistet.

Tour d'observation « Kupla »

Le HUT (Helsinki University of Technology) joue un rôle central dans le développement de l'architecture scandinave traditionnelle en bois. Les étudiants de l'école peuvent s'inscrire à l'atelier Wood Studio, où ils étudient différentes disciplines architecturales autour du bois. En 2002, le concours Wood Focus Finnland a été lancé pour une tour d'observation au zoo de Helsinki. C'est Ville Hara, un architecte finlandais international à l'œuvre prolifique, qui a conçu le projet gagnant, réalisé au Wood Studio. Plusieurs décisions importantes concernant l'architecture ont été prises sur une maquette de 2 mètres de hauteur lors de la phase de préparation. Ville Hara a choisi une forme organique et a construit un treillage en bois cintré. La tour est dotée d'une grande stabilité en tous ses points : comme une coquille d'œuf, si un endroit est affaibli, la structure dans son ensemble reste intacte.

This tower has viewing platforms at two levels and is 10 meters tall.

Dieser Turm hat Aussichtsplatt-formen auf zwei Ebenen und ist 10 m hoch.

Cette tour de dix mètres de hauteur possède des plateformes d'observation sur deux niveaux.

The wood was bent and twisted to create the bubble-like grid.

Für die blasenförmige Gitternetz-konstruktion wurden die Hölzer gebogen und in sich gedreht.

Le bois a été cintré et torsadé pour créer ce treillage en forme de bulle.

Situated on a coastal hill, the observation tower draws distant eyes toward itself.

Auf einer Anhöhe über der Meeresküste gelegen, zieht der Aussichtspunkt selbst die Blicke aus der Ferne auf sich.

Située sur une butte qui surplombe la mer, la tour d'observation est elle-même devenue un point de repère dans le paysage.

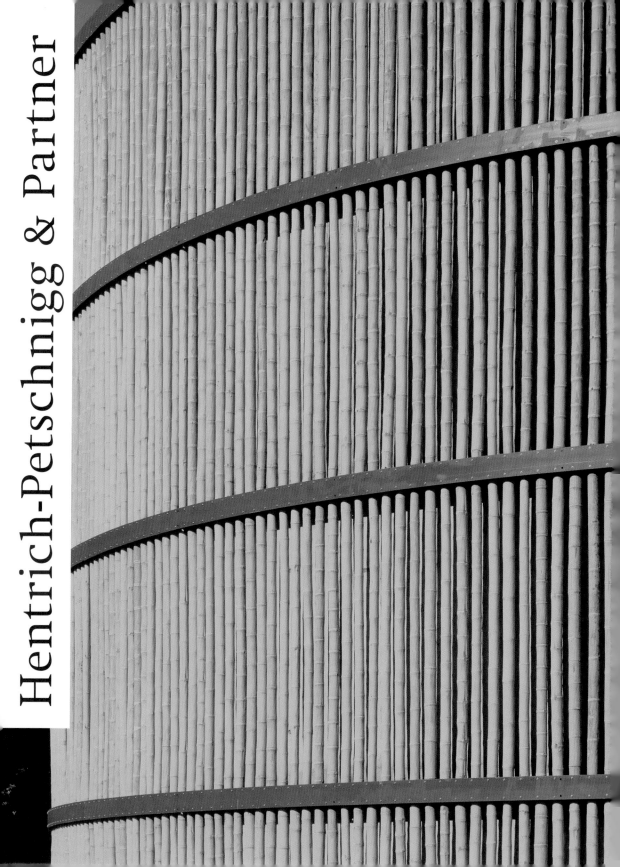

Hentrich-Petschnigg & Partner

Car Park at the zoo

Bamboo until now has been seldom used as a building material in Europe, though that could soon change. A car park planned for Leipzig Zoo was supposed to emphasize the location's natural theme and exude a certain exotic feel. The interior of the parking structure was erected from steel girders on a smoothly rounded ground plan. But from the outside neither the utilitarian structure nor the parked vehicles should be visible, so the facade was completely covered in 10-cm-thick bamboo poles. Enough light and air reach the inside of the building through the 7.5-cm spaces between bamboo poles. Pedestrians are also well served in the car park: between the bamboo wall and the parking levels is an interior walkway, allowing physical proximity to this unusual material.

Parkhaus am Zoo

Bambus ist ein in Europa bisher noch wenig genutzter Baustoff für Gebäude, was sich jedoch bald ändern könnte. Ein Parkhaus für den Leipziger Zoo sollte die Naturthematik des Ortes zum Ausdruck bringen und eine gewisse Exotik ausstrahlen. Auf weich gerundetem Grundriss wurden die Parkdecks im Inneren aus Stahlträgern errichtet. Außen sollten aber weder die zweckmäßige Konstruktion, noch die parkenden Fahrzeuge sichtbar sein, weshalb die Fassade komplett mit gut 10 cm starken Bambushalmen verkleidet wurde. Durch die Bambuszwischenräume von 7,5 cm fällt genug Licht und Luft ins Innere des Gebäudes. Auch Fußgänger kommen im Parkhaus zu ihrem Recht: Zwischen der Bambuswand und den Autodecks legte man im Gebäudeinneren Gehwege an und ermöglichte damit sogar die haptische Nähe zu diesem ungewöhnlichen Material.

Parking du zoo

Jusqu'à maintenant, le bambou n'a été utilisé que rarement dans la construction en Europe, mais cela pourrait bientôt changer. Ce parking pour le zoo de Leipzig devait accentuer la thématique naturelle du lieu et transmettre une notion d'exotisme. L'intérieur de la structure, fait de poutres en acier, se dresse sur un plan arrondi. Mais ni l'ossature fonctionnelle ni les voitures garées ne devaient être visibles de l'extérieur, c'est pourquoi la façade a été complètement recouverte de tiges de bambou de 10 centimètres d'épaisseur. Les espaces de 7,5 centimètres entre chaque tige laissent pénétrer l'air et la lumière à l'intérieur de l'édifice. Les piétons ne sont pas oubliés : un passage piéton interne situé entre le mur en bambou et les plateformes de parking leur permettent de s'approcher de ce matériau inhabituel.

The uncomfortable semi-darkness of conventional car parks is replaced by a soft, gold-toned shadow, as in a sparse forest.

Das unangenehme Halbdunkel herkömmlicher Parkhäuser entfällt hier zugunsten sanfter, goldfarbener Schatten, wie bei einem lichten Wald.

L'obscurité désagréable des parkings traditionnels est remplacée par une pénombre douce aux tons dorés, comme dans une forêt clairsemée.

Thomas Herzog

Hanover 2000 Expo Roof

This construction is an architectural creation of superlatives. At the time of its construction it was the world's largest area covered by a freestanding wooden structure, at 26 meters total height and 16,000 square meters of area. The Expo Roof consists of peaked shades joined at strategic points. The outer edges of the shades are each 20-m long. They rest on bundled wooden pillars whose corner supports consist of noble fir trunks. The appropriate trees were chosen and felled a year before construction in the southern Black Forest. Aside from the column bases and the midpoints of the shades the entire structure is of wood.

EXPO-Dach Hannover 2000

Diese Konstruktion ist eine Architektur der Superlative. Zum Zeitpunkt ihrer Errichtung war sie mit 26 m Gesamthöhe und 16.000 m² überspannter Fläche der größte freitragende Holzbau der Welt. Das EXPO-Dach besteht aus zehn Schirmen, die punktuell miteinander verknüpft sind. Die Außenkanten der Schirme haben jeweils eine Länge von 20 m. Sie ruhen auf hölzernen Pfeilerbündeln, deren Eckstützen aus halben Weißtannenbaumstämmen gebildet werden. Die entsprechenden Bäume wurden ein Jahr vor Verbauung im Südschwarzwald ausgewählt und geschlagen. Außer den Stützenfüßen und den Schirmmittelpunkten besteht die gesamte Konstruktion aus Holz.

Toit de l'EXPO de Hanovre 2000

Cette construction est une œuvre architecturale qui mérite tous les superlatifs. Avec une hauteur totale de 26 mètres et 16 000 mètres carrés, c'était au moment de sa construction la plus grande surface au monde couverte par une structure en bois indépendante. Le toit de l'EXPO est formé de dix écrans carrés de 20 mètres de côté rattachés les uns aux autres en différents points. Ils reposent sur des piliers en bois dont les coins sont formés par des moitiés de troncs de sapin blanc. Les arbres ont été sélectionnés et coupés dans le sud de la Forêt noire un an avant le début du chantier. Toute la structure est en bois, à l'exception des pieds des piliers et des points centraux des écrans.

Multiple layers of wooden lattices make up the shade surfaces.

Mehrere Schichten von Holzgittern bilden die Schirmflächen.

Les écrans sont constitués de plusieurs couches de treillages en bois.

Only the centers of the shades, which must disperse great force, are not made of wood, but instead of cast steel.

Nur die Schirmmittelpunkte, die starke Zugkräfte ausgleichen müssen, bestehen nicht aus Holz, sondern aus Gussstahl.

Seuls les centres des écrans, qui doivent supporter de grandes forces de traction, ne sont pas en bois, mais en fonte d'acier.

The Expo Roof remained after the exhibition year and is now the trademark of the Hanover Trade Fair site.

Das EXPO-Dach verblieb nach dem Ausstellungsjahr an seinem Ort und ist heute das Wahrzeichen der Messe Hannover.

Le toit de l'EXPO est resté après l'année de l'événement, et est maintenant un emblème du parc des expositions de Hanovre.

Heydorn.Eaton.Architekten

House "am Hochgericht"

A prominent historic building in the middle of the village was intended to become the new cultural center of Urbach (Germany). The understated architecture after renovating the simple freestanding building elevated it to the focal point. The spare, almost forbidding exterior of the house seems secretive and leaves the observer curious. Sidings of horizontal, untreated Douglas fir slats surround the building above the low-walled ground floor. They extend to the eaves of the roof and even cover the two windows on the gable ends. The severity of the creation is consistent with a modern design concept, but at the same time suggests the simplicity of barns. Ultimately, the house will serve as the village museum depicting local living traditions.

Haus am Hochgericht

Ein prominent in der Dorfmitte gelegenes historisches Gebäude sollte zum neuen Kulturzentrum von Urbach werden. Nach der Sanierung hat man den schlichten freistehenden Bau durch eine Architektur des Understatements zum Blickpunkt erhoben. Es ist vor allem das karge, fast abweisende Äußere des Hauses, welches geheimnisvoll wirkt und neugierig macht. Oberhalb des niedrigen gemauerten Erdgeschosses umschließt eine Verkleidung aus horizontalen, unbehandelten Douglasienvollholzbrettern das Gebäude. Sie reicht bis unter die Dachkante und läuft sogar über die beiden Fenster an den Giebelseiten hinweg. Die Strenge der Gestaltung entspricht dabei durchaus einem modernen Designkonzept, ist aber gleichzeitig als Anspielung auf schlichte Scheunenbauten gedacht. Schließlich soll das Haus als Dorfmuseum lokale Lebens- und Wohntraditionen veranschaulichen.

Maison « am Hochgericht »

Un important bâtiment historique situé au centre du village devait devenir le nouveau centre culturel communal de Urbach en Allemagne. L'élégance discrète de sa rénovation a transformé cet édifice tout simple en point de mire. L'extérieur dépouillé, presque sévère de la maison semble renfermer des secrets et éveille la curiosité. Elle est revêtue de planches horizontales de sapin de Douglas non traité au-dessus du rez-de-chaussée aux murs bas. Ce revêtement arrive jusqu'au toit et couvre même les deux fenêtres des pignons. La sévérité de la création est typique d'un concept moderne, mais elle suggère également la simplicité des granges. Finalement, cette maison sera le musée du village et illustrera les traditions locales.

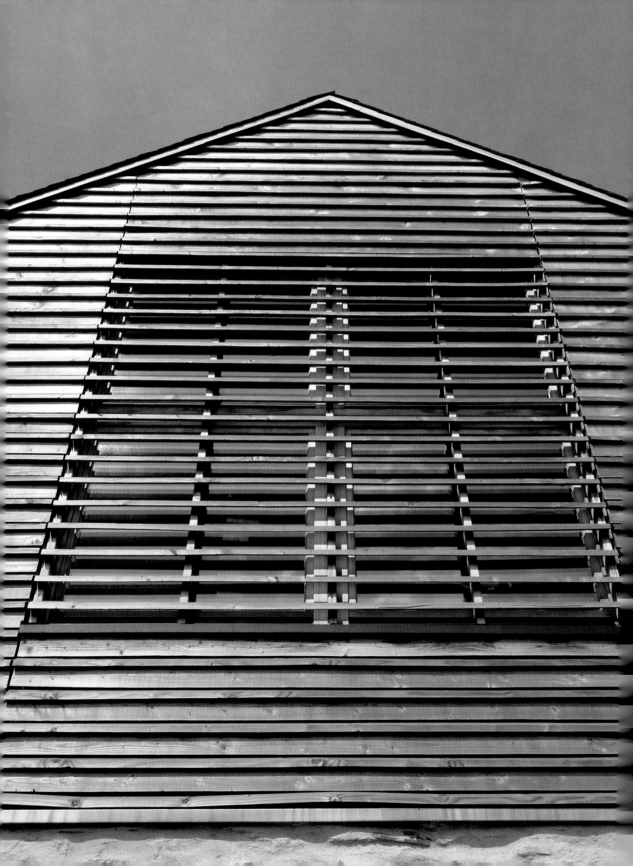

The interior rooms of the village museum are completely paneled with pine.

Die Innenräume des Dorfmuseums sind vollständig mit Kiefernholz ausgekleidet.

À l'intérieur du musée du village, les pièces sont entièrement revêtues de pin.

Jensen & Skodvin

Cistercian Mary Cloister

This structure lies on the remote Norwegian island of Tautra. Jensen & Skodvin built a new nuns' cloister here with a small church as well as rooms for work and services. A complete analysis of cloistered life found halls and other connecting passages were unnecessary, and the originally recommended usable space was reduced by a third. The individual cloister buildings touch one another. To prevent them blocking the daylight from one another, roof surfaces were opened. The church, for example, has a glass roof supported by an artistically crafted spruce frame. The room not only has enough light but is also bathed in a varied play of light that fits well with the metaphysical atmosphere of the location.

Zisterzienserinnen-Marienkloster

Das Objekt befindet sich weltabgelegen auf der Insel Tautra (Norwegen). Hier wurde ein neues Nonnenkloster mit kleiner Kirche und Wirtschafts- und Ordensräumlichkeiten von Jensen & Skodvin errichtet. Durch eingehende Analysen des Ordenslebens konnte auf Flure und andere Verbindungswege verzichtet und die ursprünglich veranschlagte Nutzfläche um ein Drittel reduziert werden. Nun grenzen die einzelnen Klostergebäude direkt aneinander. Damit sie sich nicht gegenseitig das Tageslicht nehmen, wurden Dachflächen geöffnet. Die Kirche beispielsweise erhielt ein Glasdach, welches von einem kunstvoll gezimmerten Fichtengebälk getragen wird. Nun hat der Raum nicht nur genügend Helligkeit, sondern er erscheint in ein vielfältiges Lichtspiel getaucht, das gut zur metaphysischen Atmosphäre des Ortes passt.

Couvent cistercien Sainte-Marie

Cette structure se trouve sur l'île norvégienne de Tautra, retranchée du monde. Jensen & Skodvin a construit un nouveau couvent et une petite église ainsi que de petites pièces pour les activités économiques et religieuses des nonnes. Une analyse en profondeur de la vie du couvent a révélé que les couloirs et autres lieux de passage n'étaient pas nécessaires, et l'espace utile recommandé initialement a été réduit d'un tiers. Les différents bâtiments du couvent se touchent les uns les autres. Pour éviter qu'ils ne bloquent la lumière, les surfaces des toits ont été ouvertes. Par exemple, l'église est dotée d'un toit en verre qui repose sur une charpente en épicéa très artistique. Non seulement la pièce reçoit un éclairage suffisant, mais elle est aussi baignée d'un jeu de lumière changeant en parfaite harmonie avec l'atmosphère du lieu.

In the chapel, diagonals formed
by great beams dominate the
picture – they even divide the
windows.

Im Kirchenraum beherrschen die
Diagonalen aus mächtigen Balken
das Bild – sie teilen sogar die
Fensterflächen.

Dans la chapelle, les diagonales
des grandes poutres qui divisent
les fenêtres dominent la scène.

When shadows multiply the
beams' patterns, the roof and wall
seem to run seamlessly together.

Wenn die Schatten das Muster der
Balken verdoppeln, scheinen
Dach und Wand nahtlos inein-
ander überzugehen.

Lorsque les ombres multiplient les
motifs des poutres, le toit et le
mur semblent ne faire qu'un.

The surfaces of the different woods, flagstones and copper pipes build a warm reddish-brown color palette.

Die Oberflächen der verschiedenen Hölzer, der Steinplatten und der Kupferrohre bilden gemeinsam ein warmes Rot-Braun-Farbspektrum.

Les surfaces des différentes essences de bois, des dalles en pierre et des tuyaux en cuivre forment une palette chaleureuse de bruns et de rouges.

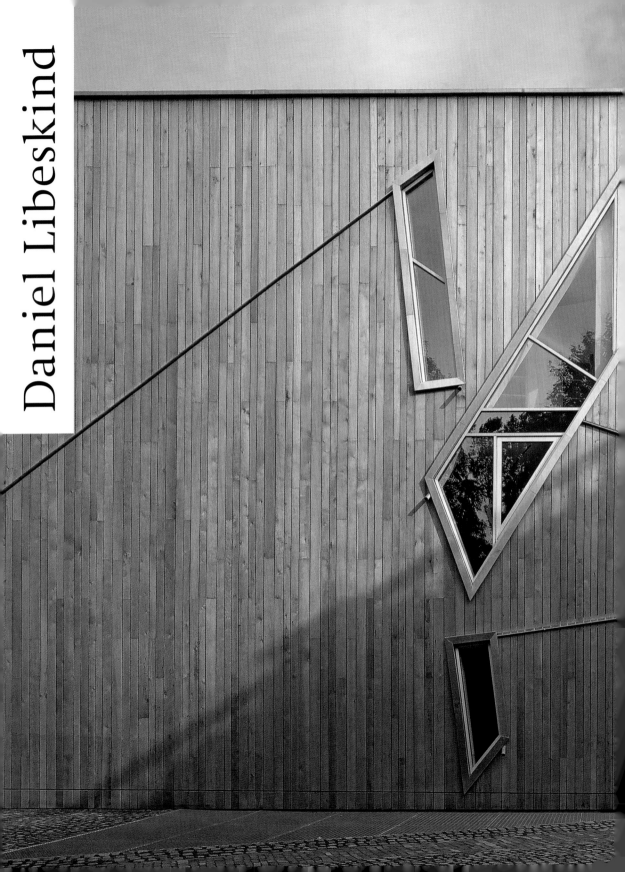

Daniel Libeskind

Felix Nussbaum Museum

The Felix Nussbaum Museum in the painter's hometown of Osnabrück (Germany) is an exhibition house and memorial to this artist who was persecuted and murdered under the Third Reich. Libeskind conceived of an ensemble of jarringly different individual buildings as a reflection of Nussbaum's chaotic life on the run. The visitor experiences the so-called 'Nussbaum Walk' of concrete and the 'Nussbaum Bridge' of zinc plate as extremely threatening. With their cold materials and dark aesthetic, they represent the time of his persecution. The 'Nussbaum House,' home to the main collection of paintings, symbolizes the still-friendly, happy early years of the artist. The architect chose wood with its lively, warm manifestation for this positive time.

Felix Nussbaum Museum

Das Museum für den Maler Felix Nussbaum in dessen Geburtsort Osnabrück ist Ausstellungshaus und Gedenkstätte dieses im Dritten Reich verfolgten und getöteten Künstlers. Libeskind konzipierte ein Ensemble aus extrem gegensätzlichen Einzelgebäuden, als Spiegel der Zerrissenheit im Flüchtlingsleben von Nussbaum. Dabei erlebt der Besucher den „Nussbaum-Gang" aus Beton und die „Nussbaum-Brücke" aus Zinkblech als äußerst bedrohlich. Sie stehen mit ihren kalten Materialien und finsteren Ästhetik für die Zeit der Verfolgung. Das „Nussbaum-Haus", welches die Hauptgemäldesammlung enthält, symbolisiert die noch freundliche, unbeschwerte frühe Lebensepoche des Künstlers. Als Material wählte der Architekt Holz, das mit seinem lebendigen, warmen Ausdruck für diese positive Zeit steht.

Musée Felix Nussbaum

Le musée du peintre Felix Nussbaum dans sa ville natale d'Osnabrück en Allegmagne est un lieu d'exposition, mais aussi d'hommage à cet artiste persécuté et assassiné sous le Troisième Reich. Daniel Libeskind a conçu un ensemble disparate de bâtiments individuels pour refléter le chaos de la vie que Nussbaum a passée en fuite. Le visiteur y fait l'expérience des très menaçants « Passage Nussbaum » en béton et « Pont Nussbaum » en feuilles de zinc. Avec leurs matériaux froids et leur esthétique sombre, ils représentent l'époque où il a été persécuté. La « Maison Nussbaum », qui abrite la collection principale de tableaux, symbolise les jeunes années encore insouciantes du peintre. L'architecte a choisi le bois et la notion de chaleur et de vie qu'il véhicule pour représenter cette époque heureuse.

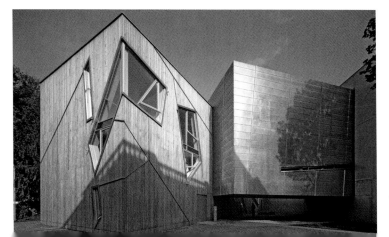

The Nussbaum Museum is one of the few buildings where this architect has used wood.

Das Nussbaum-Museum ist eines der wenigen Gebäude des Architekten, bei denen er mit Holz arbeitete.

Le musée Nussbaum est l'une des rares œuvres en bois de cet architecte.

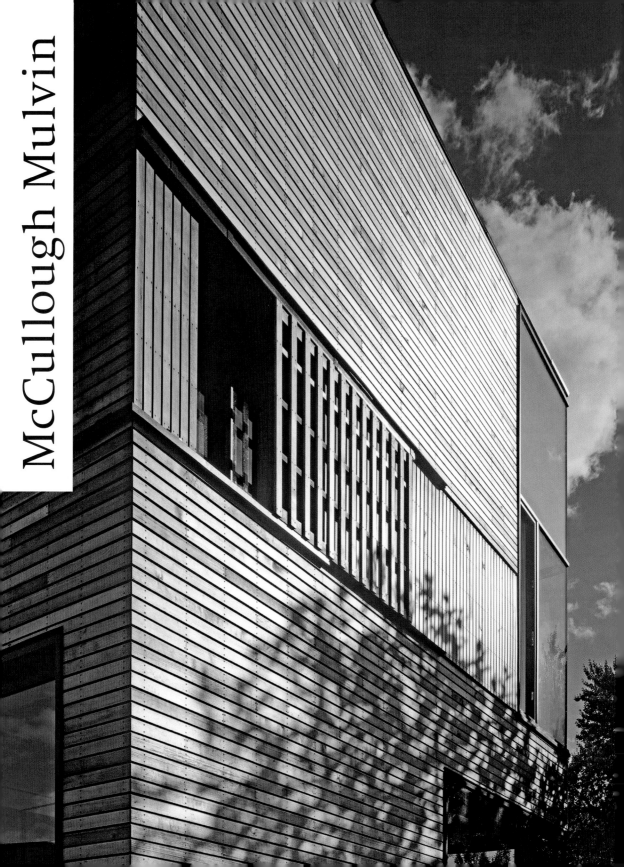

McCullough Mulvin

Virus Reference Laboratory

The elaborate aesthetic of this University of Dublin research laboratory lets it compete with the residential-building designs. Each side of the building shows a unique, almost constructivist facade arrangement. There is no recognizable norm for window size. The variations on the shape of the square as a basic shape seem limitless. It really stands out in a row of nine smaller institutional buildings on campus.

Virusreferenzlabor

In seiner ausgefeilten Ästhetik kann es dieses Forschungslabor der Universität Dublin mit dem Anspruch von Residential Building aufnehmen. Jede Gebäudeseite weist eine individuelle, quasi konstruktivistische Fassadengestaltung auf. Keine Norm für Fenstergrößen ist erkennbar. Im Spiel mit dem Rechteck als Grundform scheinen die Variationsmöglichkeiten unendlich. In einer Reihe von neun kleineren Institutsgebäuden auf dem Campus fällt es entsprechend aus dem Rahmen.

Laboratoire de référence de virologie

L'esthétique sophistiquée de ce laboratoire de recherche de l'Université de Dublin lui permet de rivaliser avec les immeubles résidentiels. Chaque côté du bâtiment présente une façade au motif unique, presque constructiviste. Les dimensions des fenêtres n'obéissent à aucune formule identifiable, et les variations sur la base du carré semblent infinies. Il prend clairement la vedette dans la rangée de neuf autres bâtiments du campus, plus petits.

The building's clear shapes work well against the background of a Japanese garden.

Vor dem Hintergrund einer japanischen Gartenanlage kommen die klaren Formen des Gebäudes gut zum Ausdruck.

Ses formes nettes sont en harmonie avec le jardin japonais qui lui sert de toile de fond.

MGF Mahler Günster Fuchs

Technical and Business College

The buildings of the colleges of electronics, optics and information technology, on a gentle slope at the edge of the woods, create an attractive ensemble. These are three long rectangular buildings, all with apparently smooth, gleaming, reddish-brown exterior surfaces of larch wood. On second glance, the sidings arrangement in three horizontal stripes becomes visible. In front of each of these three levels, pivoting vertical wooden shutters are closely spaced; the horizontal wood slats then divide each pivoting door again. Because the shutters on one interior room can be moved independently of those on other rooms, new patterns constantly emerge on the facades. Light alternates with dark and horizontal stripes follow vertical ones. When the shutters are completely open, the shiny glass inside becomes visible next to the matt wood surface.

Hochschule für Technik und Wirtschaft

Die Gebäude der Studiengänge Elektronik, Optik und Informatik bilden auf einer sanft abfallenden Fläche vor einem Waldrand ein ansprechendes Ensemble. Es handelt sich um drei lang gestreckte Baurechtecke – alle mit scheinbar vollkommen glatten, rotbraun schimmernden Außenflächen aus unbehandeltem Lärchenholz. Auf den zweiten Blick bemerkt man eine Gliederung der Holzverkleidung in drei horizontal verlaufende Streifen. Vor jeder dieser drei Etagen sind dicht an dicht gleich große, vertikal drehbare Holzjalousien angebracht; jede Drehtür wird wiederum durch ihre Horizontallamellen gegliedert. Da die zu einem Innenraum gehörenden Jalousien jeweils unabhängig von den anderen Räumen zu bewegen sind, bilden sich stets neue Muster an den Fassaden: Hell wechselt mit Dunkel und horizontale folgen auf vertikale Streifen. Bei weit ausgeklappten Jalousien wird die glänzende, innenliegende Verglasung neben der matten Holzoberfläche sichtbar.

École supérieure de technologie et d'économie

Situés sur une pente douce à la lisière d'un bois, les bâtiments des filières d'électronique, d'optique et des technologies de l'information forment un ensemble à l'esthétique séduisante. Il s'agit de trois longs bâtiments rectangulaires dont la surface extérieure en mélèze brun-rouge semble complètement lisse. Un regard plus attentif distingue cependant les trois bandes horizontales du revêtement des façades. Des volets pivotants verticaux en bois sont disposés en rangs serrés le long de chaque étage, eux-mêmes subdivisés par des lattes horizontales. Les volets de chaque pièce sont indépendants des volets des autres pièces, et de nouveaux motifs émergent constamment sur les façades. Les couleurs claires et sombres alternent, ainsi que les lignes horizontales et verticales. Lorsque les volets sont complètement ouverts, le verre brillant de l'intérieur apparaît à côté de la surface mate du bois.

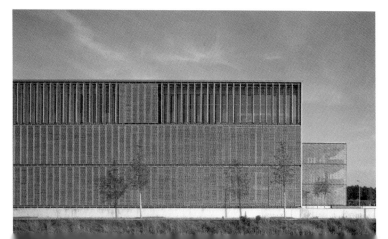

Over time, the effects of weather will convert the uniform wood facades to an even more changeable surface.

Witterungseinflüsse werden die Ebenmäßigkeit der neuen Holzfassaden mit der Zeit in eine stärker changierende Oberfläche verwandeln.

Avec le passage du temps, les façades en bois uniformes deviendront encore plus changeantes.

The interior rooms also benefit
from the fine wood, left un-
stained in its natural color.

Auch die Innenräume profitieren
von der Wirkung des edlen, in
seiner natürlichen Farbe belasse-
nen Materials Holz.

À l'intérieur, les pièces bénéficient
également de ce bois noble
dont on a conservé la couleur
naturelle.

The stairwells are situated across
the building's long axis and are lit
from above.

Die Treppenaufgänge wurden auf
dem schmalen Streifen der
Gebäudelängsachse zusammenge-
zogen und von oben belichtet.

Les cages d'escalier sont situées
sur l'axe de la longueur du
bâtiment, et sont éclairées par le
toit.

College of Design

This structure is revolutionary for the combination of wood and glass used in its construction. After developing the facade idea for this building, a completely new product was introduced, which the glass manufacturer OKALUX now markets under the name Okawood. It is a panel with real wooden slats embedded between two layers of insulating safety glass. Following extensive testing, a Dark Red Merani wood was selected for this purpose. The Okawood panels create a homogenous surface and are window and wall in one. From inside out the elements have good transparency, while they completely shield the view from outside in.

MGF also used a custom solution for the long sides of the building. A post-and-beam system creates the three stories. The system was left unfinished on the inside and kept open for use as a shelf and display area.

Fakultät für Gestaltung

Dieses Gebäude wird für die Kombination von Holz und Glas am Bau wegweisend sein. Nach der Entwicklung von Fassadenkonzepten für den Neubau ging ein völlig neues Produkt in Serie, das nun vom Glashersteller OKALUX unter dem Namen Okawood vertrieben wird. Es handelt sich dabei um ein Paneel, bei dem zwischen zwei Sicherheitsisoliergläsern Lamellen aus Echtholz fest eingebaut sind. Nach umfangreichen Tests wählte man „Dark Red Merani"-Holz für diesen Zweck aus. Die Okawood-Paneele bilden eine homogene Fläche und sind dabei Fenster und Wand in einem. Von innen nach außen haben die Elemente eine sehr gute Transparenz, während von außen nach innen vollkommener Sichtschutz gewährleistet ist.

Für die Gebäudelängsseiten haben MGF Architekten ebenfalls ein maßgeschneidertes Konzept erstellt. Ein Pfosten-Riegel-System aus Holz bildet die Geschosse. Es ist zu den Innenräumen hin nicht verblendet, sondern zur Nutzung als Regal und Ausstellungsfläche offen gelassen.

Faculté de Design

Ce bâtiment est révolutionnaire pour la combinaison de bois et de verre employée dans sa construction. Après le développement de concepts pour la façade un tout nouveau produit a été lancé, que le fabricant de verre OKALUX commercialise à présent sous le nom Okawood. Il s'agit d'un panneau où des lattes de bois massif sont montées entre deux plaques de verre isolant de sécurité. Au terme de nombreux tests, on a choisi pour ces panneaux le bois « Dark Red Merani ». Les panneaux Okawood créent une surface homogène qui est mur et fenêtre à la fois. Les éléments ont une très bonne transparence de l'intérieur vers l'extérieur, mais créent un véritable rempart visuel dans le sens contraire.

Les architectes de MGF ont également utilisé une solution sur mesure pour les grands côtés du bâtiment. Les trois étages se créent autour d'un système de montants et de traverses. Ce système n'a pas été paré à l'intérieur, et a été laissé à découvert de façon à servir d'étagère et de surface d'exposition.

Vertically hinged windows
mounted edge to edge were used
for the exterior finish.

Als äußere Gebäudehaut wurden
vertikal klappbare Fenster auf
Stoß montiert.

Des fenêtres à bascule verticales,
montées bord à bord, font office
de revêtement extérieur.

In front of the building is a small
oak grove for which the depart-
ment is named. It provides light
shade like the Okawood system.

Vor dem Gebäude befindet sich
ein Eichenhain, nach dem die
Fakultät benannt ist. Er spendet
lichten Schatten, so wie das
Okawood-System.

Ce sont les chênes qui se trouvent
devant le bâtiment qui donnent
son nom à la faculté. Ils donnent
des ombres légères, tout comme le
système Okawood.

Nils Holger Moormann

Berge Guesthouse

In a manner of speaking, the berge Guesthouse is the habitable corporate identity of the Nils Holger Moormann design studio. When it was time to expand the corporate headquarters, the firm had acquired a 400-year-old farmstead in need of restoration and decided not to tear it down. Piece by piece, the building's structure was uncovered and restored to a state worthy of historical preservation – a process that is continuing. As the interior rooms become usable, Nils Holger Moormann has an entire house in which to develop and apply his interior-design ideas. Fittingly, the rooms are not only decorated with existing Moormann furniture, but also the modular systems he has designed are being further developed here. In addition, nearly every room has unique new built-ins. Most of the furniture is wood in the form of laminated lumber-core plywood (primarily birch and MDF). The house is used for experimentation, as a shop and exhibition space, but also as a guesthouse for friends and interested parties.

Gästehaus „berge"

Wenn man so will, entsteht mit Gästehaus „berge" gerade die bewohnbare Corporate Identity des Designbüros Nils Holger Moormann. Bei der Ausweitung des Firmenstandortes war man in den Besitz eines 400 Jahre alten baufälligen Gehöftes gekommen und entschied sich zunächst einmal gegen dessen Abriss. Nach und nach wurde die Gebäudesubstanz entdeckt und denkmalgerecht in Stand gesetzt – ein Prozess, der noch in Gang ist. Mit den entstehenden Innenräumen steht Nils Holger Moormann nun auch ein ganzes Haus zur Entwicklung und Anwendung seiner Interior-Design-Themen zur Verfügung. Entsprechend sind die Räume nicht nur mit vorhandenen Moormann-Möbeln ausgestattet, sondern die von ihm entwickelten Modulsysteme werden hier weiter variiert. Darüber hinaus erhält fast jeder Raum individuelle neue Einbauten. Zentrales Material der Möbel ist Holz in Form von beschichteten Tischlerplatten (vornehmlich Birkensperrholz und MDF). Das Haus wird als Experimentierfeld, Werkstatt, Ausstellungsfläche und als Gästehaus genutzt.

Maison d'invités « berge »

La maison d'invités « berge » est en quelque sorte une expression habitable de l'image d'entreprise du studio de design de Nils Holger Moormann. L'entreprise a acheté pour son projet d'agrandissement une ferme vieille de 4 siècles qui tombait en ruine, et a finalement décidé de ne pas la démolir. Peu à peu, la structure du bâtiment a été dégagée et restaurée comme un véritable monument historique. Ce processus se poursuit encore à ce jour. Au fur et à mesure que les pièces deviennent utilisables, Nils Holger Moormann dispose de toute une maison pour développer et appliquer ses idées d'aménagement. Non seulement ces pièces sont décorées avec des meubles de sa collection existante, mais il les utilise pour poursuivre le développement de ses systèmes modulaires. Chaque pièce est en outre dotée d'éléments intégrés uniques. La plupart des meubles sont en contreplaqué à âme en bois (bouleau et MDF principalement). La maison sert de terrain d'expérimentation, d'atelier et d'espace d'exposition, mais aussi de maison d'invités pour les amis et les relations d'affaires.

Excellently crafted masonry and carpentry work stands on its own and needs no painting over.

Exzellent gearbeitetes Maurer- und Tischlerhandwerk steht für sich und bedarf keinerlei Übermalung.

La qualité des travaux de maçon- nerie et de menuiserie se suffit à elle-même et ne nécessite aucune couche de peinture.

Old floorboards were preserved like treasures – new ones still need to develop a patina.

Alte Dielen wurden wie Schätze aufbewahrt – die neuen müssen ihre Patina erst erwerben.

Les vieilles planches du parquet ont été préservées comme des trésors. Les nouvelles doivent encore se faire une patine.

Wood and full-tone colors bring old and new together in "berge".

Holz und satte Farbtöne führen im Gästehaus „berge" Alt und Neu zusammen.

Le bois et les couleurs saturées marient passé et présent sous le toit de la maison « berge ».

Walden Garden Structure

Walden is not clearly either a house or a piece of furniture. This structure, appointed with incredible wit, tells the story of someone who enjoys being in the garden, but wants to have everything needed for idleness and erudition at hand without constantly having to run back and forth. In fact, many of these things are included in Walden supplies: garden tools, grill, seat cushions, flowerpots, suet, dustpan and beer glasses. Other things are built-in, like the table, bench and sunroof. But Walden is indeed a sort of house, because it has a closet, seating and sleeping areas, and even a second floor. Aside from that it is simply a delightful work of art – from the side put together like a picture and on the whole made like a sculpture. Its name is derived from the Henry David Thoreau novella *Walden*.

Gartenobjekt „Walden"

Walden ist nicht eindeutig Haus noch Möbel. Das mit unglaublichem Witz ausgestatte „Objekt" erzählt die Geschichte von jemandem, der gerne im Garten ist, jedoch alle Dinge für Müßiggang und Erbauung bei sich haben möchte, ohne andauernd hin und her laufen zu müssen. Tatsächlich sind viele dieser Dinge in einer Walden-Lieferung inbegriffen: Gartengeräte, Grill, Sitzkissen, Blumentopf, Maisenknödel, Kehrblech und Biergläser. Anderes ist fest eingebaut, wie die Brotzeitklappe, die Sitzbank oder das Schiebedach. Aber eine Art Haus ist „Walden" doch, denn es besitzt Schrank, Sitz- und Schlafplatz und sogar eine zweite Etage. Davon abgesehen ist es einfach ein herrliches Kunstobjekt – von der Seite wie ein Bild und im Ganzen wie eine Skulptur aufgefasst. Sein Name leitet sich von Henry David Thoreaus Erzählung *Walden. Über das Leben in den Wäldern* her.

Structure de jardin « Walden »

Le Walden n'est ni une maison, ni un meuble. Cette « structure » incroyablement astucieuse raconte l'histoire de quelqu'un qui aime être dans le jardin, mais veut avoir à portée de main tous les accessoires nécessaires à l'oisiveté et à l'érudition sans devoir courir à droite et à gauche. Le Walden fournit d'ailleurs un bon nombre de ces objets : outils de jardinage, barbecue, coussins, pots de fleurs, graines pour les oiseaux, pelle et verres à bière. D'autres éléments sont intégrés à la structure, comme la table, le banc ou le store. Mais finalement, peut-être que le Walden est bien une sorte de maison, puisqu'il est doté d'un placard, d'espaces pour s'asseoir et pour dormir, et même d'un deuxième étage. C'est tout simplement une magnifique œuvre d'art, conçue comme une image lorsqu'on le voit de côté, mais construite comme une sculpture. Son nom vient du roman de Henry David Thoreau, *Walden ou la Vie dans les bois.*

Walden's exterior shell consists of larch, a frequently used wood for exterior architecture.

Aus Lärchenholz, einem sehr häufig verwendeten Holz im Architekturaußenbereich, besteht auch Waldens äußere Hülle.

La coque externe du Walden est en mélèze, une essence très utilisée en extérieur.

For every summer day, a new idea.

Für jeden Sommertag eine eigene Idee.

Une idée pour chaque jour d'été.

MVRDV

WoZoCo Assisted Living Apartments

The WoonZorgComplex commission planned the transition of a housing development for seniors in their fifties and sixties into a uniform building complex with fixed apartments. Because the available lot did not cover enough area, the MVRDV studio added on. Not on the ground floor or the roof though, but rather from the middle of the facade, using blocks that jut into space and look like pulled-out drawers. The complete wood siding gives the complex a uniform look that is well suited to incorporate both the old and new parts of the building, while providing a friendlier feeling. The material infuses color into the project and it is intensified through the colorful Plexiglas balconies. Perhaps this is a last hurrah of Bauhaus and De Stijl, though somewhat toned down.

WoZoCo Seniorenwohnungen

Der Auftrag „Woonzorgcomplex" sah die Überführung einer Wohnsiedlung der 1950er- und 1960er- Jahre in einen einheitlichen Gebäudekomplex mit festgelegten Wohneinheiten vor. Da die zur Verfügung stehende Grundfläche dafür nicht ausreichte, baute MVRDV „an". Allerdings nicht im Parterre oder am Dach, sondern mitten aus der Fassade heraus, mit weit auskragenden Blöcken, die wie ausgezogene Schubläden aussehen. Ein einheitliches neues Gesicht erhielt der Komplex durch die umfassende Holzverkleidung, die gut geeignet ist, die lineare Struktur der alten und neuen Gebäudeteile aufzunehmen, ihr aber eine freundlichere Ausstrahlung verleiht. Das Material bringt zudem Farbe ins Spiel, was noch gesteigert wird durch die bunten neuen Plexiglasbalkone. Vielleicht ist dies ein letzter Nachklang von Bauhaus und De Stijl, jedoch in weniger strenger Auffassung.

Résidences pour séniors WoZoCo

La commission du « Woonzorgcomplex » a planifié la transformation d'un lotissement pour les séniors d'une cinquantaine ou une soixantaine d'années en un complexe uniforme d'appartements obéissant à des spécifications bien précises. Le terrain disponible ne couvrant pas une surface suffisante, MVRDV a « ajouté » ce qui manquait. Non pas au rez-de-chaussée, ni sur le toit, mais plutôt au milieu de la façade, avec des blocs qui font saillie et ressemblent à des tiroirs ouverts. Le revêtement extérieur en bois, omniprésent, donne au complexe un nouveau visage uniforme et plus convivial, parfait pour unifier les parties anciennes et nouvelles. La couleur que ce matériau donne au projet est encore renforcée par les balcons en plexiglas multicolore. Il s'agit peut-être d'un dernier écho du Bauhaus et de De Stijl, dans une version plus modérée.

The apartments in the jutting
cubes are desirable because of the
view.

Die Wohnungen in den auskragenden Gebäudekuben sind
wegen ihrer Aussicht begehrt.

Les appartements situés dans les
cubes sont très convoités, à cause
de leurs vues.

Aluminum and sheet glass are
superimposed on one of the long
sides of the facade.

Auf einer der Längsseiten wurden
der Fassade Laubengänge aus
Aluminium und Klarglas vorgeblendet.

Des galeries couvertes en aluminium et en plaques de verre ont
été superposées à la façade de l'un
des grands côtés de l'immeuble.

Nägeliarchitekten

Forest Houses

The architects erected five very narrow houses, some on stilts, to preserve the tree stock on this small forest lot. As little ground as possible was to be built up. The tower-like buildings fit well among the close-growing tree trunks. The pattern of the larch boards on the facade, whose vertical strips are easily visible from a distance, helps the buildings blend into the trees. Within these strips, the panels are laid on the diagonal in a herringbone pattern, which won the community the name 'parquet houses.' The buildings were constructed using energy-saving methods and some have roof plantings. The modular system facilitates building one house per day.

Waldhäuser

Unter Beibehaltung des Baumbestandes in diesem kleinen Waldgrundstück errichteten die Architekten fünf sehr schlanke, teils auf Stützen gestellte Häuser. Möglichst wenig Grundfläche sollte bebaut werden. Die turmartigen Gebäude passen sich gut den dicht stehenden Baumstämmen an. Dazu trägt auch das Verlegemuster der Fassade aus Lärchenholzbrettern bei, deren Längsstreifen aus der Entfernung gut erkennbar sind. Innerhalb dieser Streifen sind die Paneele diagonal als Fischgrätmuster verlegt, was der Siedlung den Namen „Parketthäuser" einbrachte. Die Anlage wurde in Niedrigenergiebauweise errichtet und verfügt teilweise über begrünte Dächer. Das Modulsystem ermöglichte den Aufbau jeweils eines Hauses an einem Tag.

Résidences dans les bois

Les architectes ont construit cinq bâtiments très étroits, dont certains sur pilotis, pour préserver les arbres de ce petit terrain boisé. Il fallait que la surface construite soit aussi réduite que possible. Les bâtiments, semblables à des tours, s'intègrent bien à leur environnement de troncs d'arbres serrés. Le motif des planches de mélèze des façades, dont les bandes verticales sont visibles de loin, contribue à fondre les bâtiments dans les arbres. À l'intérieur de ces bandes, les panneaux sont posés en diagonale et forment des chevrons, ce qui a valu au complexe son nom de « maisons parquet ». Les bâtiments ont été construits selon des principes d'économie d'énergie et certains ont des toits végétaux. Le système modulaire a permis de construire un bâtiment par jour.

Windows are primarily on the southern exposures of the houses for passive solar-energy use.

Für die passive Sonnenenergienutzung wurden Fensterflächen hauptsächlich auf die Südseiten der Häuser konzentriert.

Le projet utilise l'énergie solaire passive, c'est pourquoi les fenêtres sont principalement orientées vers le sud.

The widths of the stripes of paneling mirror the distance between the interior vertical studs, visible behind the wide windows.

Die Streifenbreite der Holzvertäfelung gibt den Abstand der innenliegenden vertikalen Stüzen wieder, welche hinter den breiteren Fenstern sichtbar werden.

La largeur des bandes du revêtement extérieur correspond à la distance entre les montants verticaux internes, visibles derrière les grandes fenêtres.

Renzo Piano

Jean-Marie Tjibaou Cultural Center

These wooden structures are world architecture. They unite a traditional approach to building closely tied to nature with the most modern technologies. On top of that, one of the most important architects in the West created a building icon of the 21st century here in the Pacific. The landscape, with its luxuriant island groups, creates a moving background for the aesthetic monumentalism of the structures. Ten buildings with the fronts in alignment and in groupings of so-called villages form one row. The cultural center of the Kanak people houses exhibition pavilions, a library, theater and studios. These roundhouses are modeled on the native 'Great House' in their basic form and structure. Renzo Piano combined hard Iroko wood and glass over a substructure of steel. The buildings are earthquake- and storm proof and use light winds in the ventilation systems.

Kulturzentrum Jean-Marie Tjibaou

Diese Holzbauten sind Weltarchitektur. Sie vereinen eine traditionelle, ganz der Natur verbundene Bauauffassung mit modernster Technik. Zudem erschuf einer der bedeutendsten Architekten des Westens hier im Pazifik eine Bauikone des 21. Jahrhunderts. Nicht zuletzt vor dem bewegenden Hintergrund der Landschaft mit ihren üppigen Inselgruppen zeigt die Anlage eine ästhetische Monumentalität. Zehn Gebäude mit gleicher Ausrichtung der Stirnseiten und jeweils in Gruppen zu sogenannten Dörfern zusammengefasst, bilden eine Reihe. Das Kulturzentrum der kanakischen Bevölkerung beherbergt hier Ausstellungspavillons, eine Bibliothek, ein Theater und Ateliers. In ihrer Grundform und Struktur sind die Rundbauten an das einheimische „Große Haus" angelehnt. Hartes Irokoholz wurde von Renzo Piano mit Glas auf einer Unterkonstruktion aus Stahl kombiniert. Die Bauten sind erdbeben- und sturmsicher und nutzen leichte Winde innerhalb ihres Belüftungssystems.

Centre culturel Jean-Marie Tjibaou

Ces structures en bois sont ce que l'on pourrait appeler de l'architecture du monde. Elles unissent une approche traditionnelle de la construction, très proche de la nature, aux technologies les plus modernes. De plus, l'un des architectes occidentaux les plus prestigieux a créé ici, dans le Pacifique, une œuvre emblématique du XXIᵉ siècle. Les archipels luxuriants forment une toile de fond spectaculaire pour l'esthétique monumentale de ces structures. Le projet est constitué d'une rangée de dix édifices aux façades alignées regroupés en « villages ». Le centre culturel du peuple kanak abrite des pavillons d'exposition, une bibliothèque, un théâtre et des ateliers. La forme de base et la structure de ces bâtiments ronds reprennent le principe de la « grande maison » traditionnelle locale. Renzo Piano a combiné du bois d'iroko et du verre sur une ossature en acier. Les bâtiments résistent aux tremblements de terre et aux tempêtes, et leur système de ventilation tire parti des brises naturelles.

Renzo Piano, prize winner of the Spirit of Nature Wood Architecture Award 2000, built different structures of organic curved lumber-core plywood girders in Europe, i.e. the Paul Klee Museum.

Renzo Piano, Preisträger des Spirit of Nature Wood Architecture Award 2000, baute in Europa verschiedene Strukturen aus organisch gewölbten Schichtholzträgern, wie z. B. das Paul-Klee-Museum.

Renzo Piano, lauréat du prix Spirit of Nature Wood Architecture en 2000, a construit plusieurs structures sur des supports en bois cintré, par exemple le musée Paul Klee.

State Mission

A building that shows much of itself and reveals how it functions must be as open as this state mission in Berlin. The glass cube allows a view of the incorporated wood structure. Large parabolic curved beams build the vertical support structure. Further innovative bonuses of the architecture are the special, newly developed wood elements for ceiling building. The state North Rhine-Westphalia awarded this project as a programmatic commission. The architectural solution included principles of ecology, future viability and sustainability, and was meant to reflect this in the formal implementation.

Landesvertretung

Ein Gebäude, das viel von sich zeigen will, das erkennen lässt, wie es funktioniert, muss so offen sein wie diese Bundeslandvertretung in Berlin. Der Glaskubus erlaubt den Durchblick auf den eingestellten Baukörper aus Holz. Große parabelförmig gewölbte Balken bilden die vertikale Stützkonstruktion. Spezielle, neu entwickelte Holzelemente für den Deckenbau sind ein weiterer innovativer Pluspunkt der Architektur. Das Bundesland Nordrhein-Westfalen hatte das Projekt als programmatischen Auftrag vergeben. Die architektonische Lösung war an die Prinzipien der Ökologie, Zukunftsfähigkeit und Nachhaltigkeit gebunden und sollte diese in ihrer formalen Umsetzung ablesbar machen.

Délégation

Ce bâtiment se dévoile beaucoup : il révèle son fonctionnement et doit être aussi ouvert que la délégation du land à Berlin. Le cube en verre permet de voir la structure en bois intégrée. La structure porteuse verticale est formée de grandes poutres cintrées paraboliques. Les éléments en bois du plafond, conçus tout spécialement pour le projet, sont une innovation supplémentaire. Ce bâtiment est une commande programmatique du land de la Rhénanie-du-Nord-Westphalie. La solution architecturale se base sur des principes d'écologie, de flexibilité face aux besoins futurs et de durabilité, et devait refléter ces concepts dans sa réalisation formelle.

The wooden pointed arches brace the steel construction that resides within.

Die hölzernen Spitzbögen bewirken eine Aussteifung der innen liegenden Stahlkonstruktion.

Les arches pointues en bois portent la construction en acier de l'intérieur.

Reitermann / Sassenroth

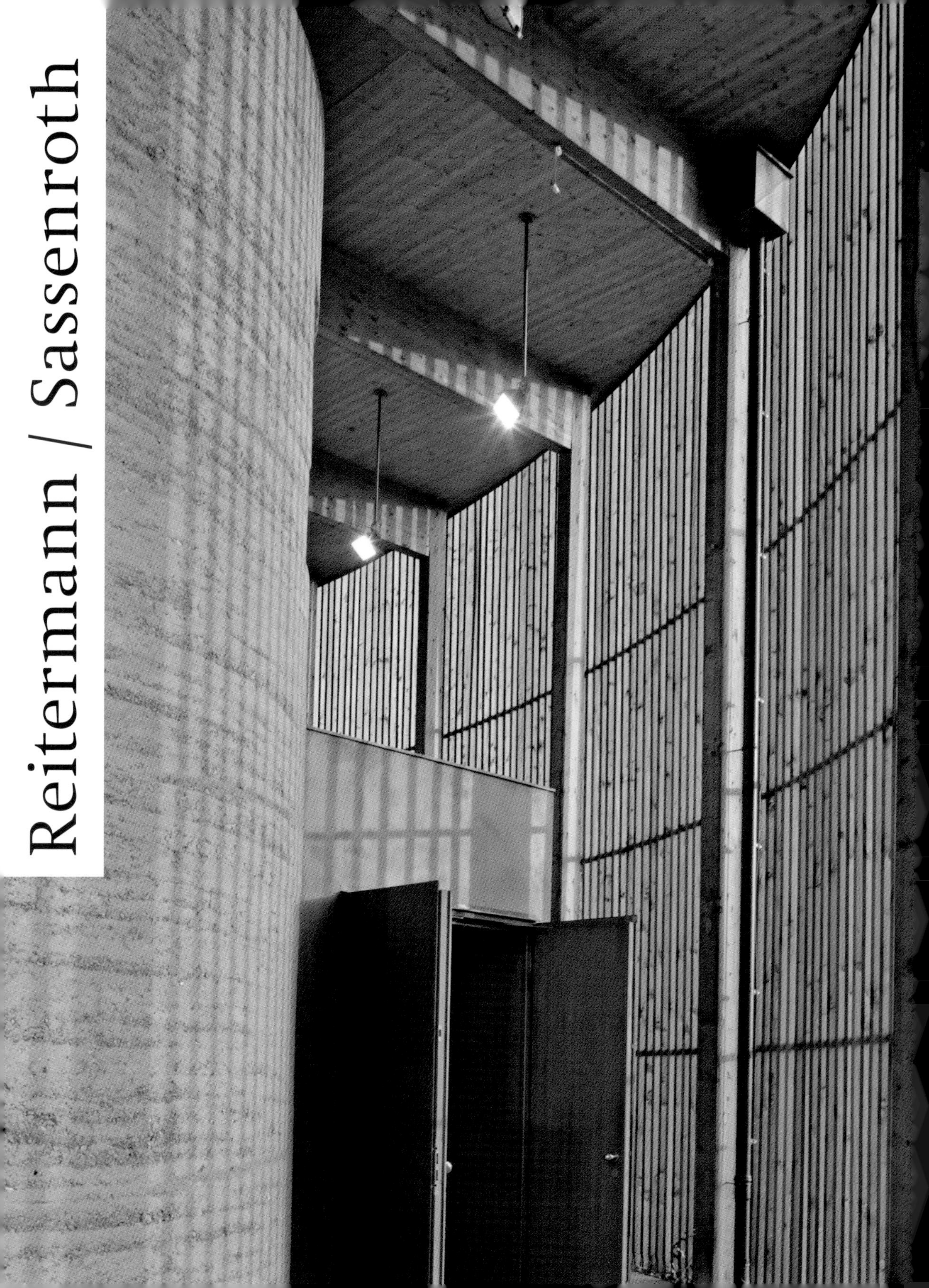

Chapel of Reconciliation

The big contemporary idea of
the wood slat facade, otherwise
frequently used on cubical
buildings, unfolds its effect on a
circular building. Viewed from a
distance, slats emphasize the malleable form of a building through
the soft amplification of the
progression of light and shadow.
They have fabric-like qualities
– from a short distance they show
a restrained, elegant structure
and allow light to shine in from
outside. The impression of the
materials immediately captivates
the visitor in this building. The
slats of unfinished Douglas fir
show their raw surface and strong
grain. The actual chapel with its
oval border of rammed clay can
be reached from the surrounding
wood wall. The previous church
on this location stood in the
prohibited area near the Berlin
Wall. The new building is not only
a community church, but also a
documentations and memorial
site for the Berlin Wall.

Kapelle der Versöhnung

Das große zeitgenössische Thema
der Holzlamellenfassade, sonst
häufig auf kubische Baukörper
angewendet, entfaltet diesmal bei
einem Rundbau seine Wirkung.
Aus der Entfernung betrachtet
heben Lamellen immer die plas-
tische Form einer Architektur
durch sanfte Verstärkung des
Licht-Schattenverlaufs hervor.
Sie haben textile Eigenschaften
– zeigen auf kurze Distanz eine
zurückhaltende, elegante Struktur und lassen Licht von außen
nach innen durchscheinen. In
diesem Gebäude nimmt den
Besucher auch der unmittelbare
Materialeindruck gefangen. Die
Lamellen aus unbehandeltem
Douglasienholz zeigen ihre raue
Oberfläche und starke Maserung.
Von der umgebenden Holzwand
gelangt man in den eigentlichen
Kirchenraum mit seiner ovalen
Umgrenzung aus Stampflehm.
Die Vorgängerkirche hatte an
dieser Stelle im Sperrgebiet der
Berliner Mauer gestanden. Der
Neubau ist nicht nur Gemeinde-
gotteshaus, sondern auch Doku-
mentations- und Gedenkstätte
der Berliner Mauer.

Chapelle de la Réconciliation

Le concept furieusement contem-
porain de la façade en lattes de
bois, souvent employé sur les
bâtiments cubiques, déploie ici ses
effets sur un bâtiment circulaire.
Observées d'une certaine distance, les lattes soulignent toujours
la plastique d'un bâtiment en
amplifiant subtilement les chan-
gements des ombres et de la lumière. Elles se comportent comme
un tissu : de près, elles révèlent
leur structure sobre et élégante,
et elles laissent la lumière de l'extérieur briller vers l'intérieur. Ici,
le visiteur est immédiatement cap-
tivé par l'impression immédiate
que transmettent les matériaux.
Les lattes en sapin de Douglas non
traité affichent leur surface brute
et leurs veines marquées. Le mur
d'enceinte en bois mène à la chapelle et à sa bordure ovale en terre
pisée. L'ancienne église qui s'éle-
vait à cet emplacement se trouvait
dans la zone interdite du mur de
Berlin. Le nouveau bâtiment est
non seulement une église communautaire, mais aussi un site de
documentation et de commémora-
tion du mur de Berlin.

The wooden exterior surface is hung in front of the building from the roof. It is not a load-bearing wall.

Die hölzerne Außenhaut ist dem Gebäude vom Dach aus vorge-hängt. Eine tragende Funktion hat sie nicht.

La surface extérieure en bois est accrochée au toit. Ce n'est pas un mur porteur.

Richard Rogers

Law Courts

This incomparable building complex in Bordeaux captivates virtually everyone who even briefly visits the court. The towering courtrooms lit from above communicate a feeling of authority. Without electronic amplification, the clever acoustics of the wonderful wooden interior carry the spoken word to every corner. The judges enter the rooms from hallways that are higher than those from which other participants and the public enter. An awe-inspiring moment arises from the fact that the buildings' purpose is not apparent at first glance, but rather its appearance calls up vague associations with houses of prayer, factories or grain silos. The combination of the more futuristic structures, like the glassed-in administrative wing, the catwalks and the roof construction with warm sculptural wood forms, is typical of Rogers. He sees no contradictions in these, so long as specific functions like good air conditioning are also fulfilled.

Landgericht

Dieser unvergleichliche Gebäudekomplex in Bordeaux zieht wohl jeden in Bann, der das Gericht vorübergehend aufsucht. Die turmhohen, von oben belichteten Verhandlungsräume vermitteln ein Gefühl von Autorität. Ohne elektronische Verstärkung trägt die ausgeklügelte Akkustik der wunderschönen hölzernen Innenausstattung das gesprochene Wort in jeden Winkel. Die Richter betreten die Räume von höher gelegenen Fluren aus, als die anderen Teilnehmer und das Publikum. Ein erfurchtgebietender Moment ergibt sich zudem aus der Tatsache, dass die Gebäude nicht auf den ersten Blick hinsichtlich ihrer Funktion erfassbar sind, vielmehr unklare Assoziationen mit alten Kultstätten, Fabriken oder Getreidesilos wecken. Die Kombination aus eher technoiden Strukturen wie dem verglasten Verwaltungstrakt, den Laufstegen und der Dachkonstruktion mit warmen skulpturalen Holzformen ist typisch für Rogers. Für ihn besteht darin kein Widerspruch, solange hier wie dort bestimmte Funktionen erfüllt werden.

Tribunal de grande instance

Ce complexe incomparable captive tous les visiteurs du tribunal à Bordeaux, même ceux qui ne font que passer. Les tours des salles de tribunal éclairées par le toit transmettent un sentiment d'autorité. L'acoustique astucieuse des magnifiques intérieurs en bois transporte la voix dans tous les recoins sans amplification électronique. Les juges entrent dans les salles par des couloirs plus élevés que ceux qu'empruntent les autres participants et le public. L'admiration surgit du fait que la fonction de ce bâtiment n'est pas évidente au premier coup d'œil. Son aspect évoque plutôt des associations lointaines avec un lieu de culte, une usine ou des réservoirs à grains. La combinaison avec d'autres éléments plus futuristes, comme l'aile administrative en verre, les passerelles et le toit en bois aux formes sculpturales et chaudes est typique de Richard Rogers. Il n'y voit pas de contradiction, du moment que les fonctions spécifiques, comme une climatisation efficace, sont assurées.

The seven cone-shaped courtrooms have uniform coverings of
red cedar.

Die kegelförmigen sieben
Gerichtssäle tragen außen eine
ebenmäßige Ummantelung aus
Rotzeder.

Les sept salles de tribunal coni-
ques sont pourvues d'un revêtement uniforme en cèdre.

The interiors of the courtrooms
are of maple.

Für die Innenausstattung der
Verhandlungsräume wurde Ahorn
verwendet.

Les intérieurs des salles de
tribunal sont en érable.

Rogers' 'justice factory' retains its spectacular ability to make a statement even alongside the city towers from the Middle Ages.

Rogers' „Rechtsprechungsfabrik" behält auch in Nachbarschaft mit den mittelalterlichen Stadttürmen ihre spektakuläre Ausdruckskraft.

Cette « usine de la justice » de Richard Rogers ne perd rien de sa force d'expression, même à côté des tours du Moyen-Âge de la ville.

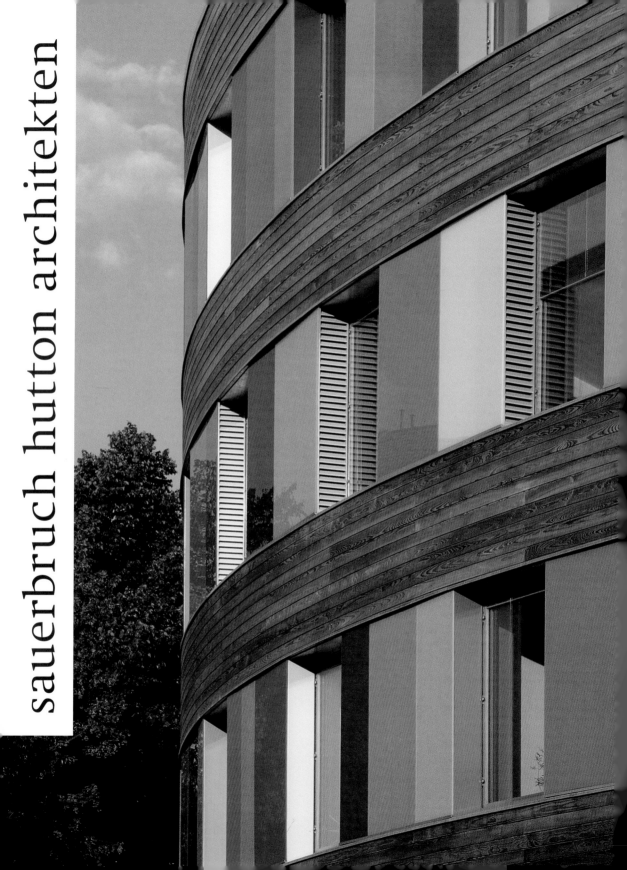

sauerbruch hutton architekten

Federal Environmental Agency

That the Federal Environmental Agency's new office at Dessau was conceived with the most current information regarding ecology is also evident in the choice of building materials. Within certain controlled parameters, wood is one of the most renewable raw materials and also has excellent room-insulating qualities. The Agency is unique in terms of the scale of building with wood in Germany. In behind-the-scenes areas there are large sub-construction systems built of wood. In addition, the window frame systems and the bands of the facade that lie between them are made of weather-resistant larch. These horizontal wood boards indicate the different floors – it is noteworthy that wood is not used to emphasize or symbolize the vertical load-bearing structures as is usual.

Umweltbundesamt

Dass die neue Niederlassung des Umweltbundesamtes in Dessau nach aktuellem ökologischen Kenntnisstand konzipiert wurde, ist auch an der Wahl der Baumaterialien ablesbar. Holz gehört innerhalb bestimmter kontrollierter Gewinnungsgrenzen zu den erneuerbaren Rohstoffen und besitzt zudem hervorragende raumklimatische Eigenschaften. Das Gebäude ist im Hinblick auf die Größenordnung der Verbauung von Holz für Deutschland einzigartig. In den nicht-sichtbaren Bereichen sind es große Unterkonstruktionssysteme, die hier aus Holz erstellt wurden. Zudem wurden die Fensterrahmensysteme und die zwischen ihnen liegenden Fassadenbänder in Holz gearbeitet, letztere aus wetterbeständigem Lärchenholz. Diese horizontal liegenden Holzleisten markieren den Etagenverlauf – es ist recht bemerkenswert, dass Holz dabei nicht zur Betonung bzw. Symbolisierung der vertikal tragenden Gebäudeteile verwendet wird, wie sonst gewöhnlich.

Agence fédérale pour l'environnement

Le choix des matériaux montre sans équivoque que les nouveaux bureaux de l'Agence fédérale pour l'environnement à Dessau ont été conçus sur la base des informations les plus actuelles sur l'écologie. Dans le cadre d'une bonne gestion forestière, le bois est l'un des matériaux les plus renouvelables. Il possède également d'excellentes propriétés isolantes. L'Agence est unique en Allemagne en termes de dimensions d'une construction en bois. Les espaces dissimulés à la vue abritent de grands systèmes d'ossature en bois. Les encadrements des fenêtres et les bandes qui les séparent sur la façade sont également en bois, ces dernières en mélèze résistant aux intempéries. Ces planches horizontales indiquent les différents étages. Contrairement à ce qui est habituel, ici le bois n'est pas utilisé pour souligner ou symboliser les structures porteuses verticales.

The two buildings are more open on the sides that face the long, stretched-out atrium.

Zu ihrem langgestreckten Atrium hin sind die beiden Gebäudestreifen stärker geöffnet.

Les deux bâtiments sont plus ouverts sur les côtés qui font face à l'atrium, tout en longueur.

Summer House

This vacation home was actually a private undertaking of the young architects and intended only for personal use. With this apprentice piece, they found concise style elements with wood that attracted the attention of professionals in the field and invitations to larger contests. The small ensemble is characterized from a few strong lines, including an elegantly rounded shape. This is a result of what the owners do here: they settle on the edge of the forest to enjoy the view of the powerful fjord. The rounded sides of the pavilion provide a protective backrest as with a beach cabana. The residents can take in their unique view while walking on the spacious patio that stretches away from the little house, parallel to the fjord. The wood deck is carefully laid around large tree trunks, making the small house appear to be rooted in the forest.

Sommerhaus

Eigentlich war das Ferienhaus ein privates Vorhaben der jungen Architekten und nur zur eigenen Nutzung bestimmt. Mit dieser Fingerübung fanden sie allerdings zu einer prägnanten Formensprache in Holz, die ihnen die Aufmerksamkeit der Bauwelt und Einladungen zu größeren Wettbewerben einbrachte. Das kleine Ensemble wird geprägt von wenigen Linien, darunter eine elegant gerundete Form. Diese ergibt sich aus dem, was die Bewohner hier tun: Man lässt sich am Waldrand nieder, um den Blick über den beeindruckenden Fjord zu genießen. Wie bei einem Strandkorb bildet die gerundete Pavillonseite eine schützende Rückenlehne. Parallel zum Fjord erstreckt sich vom Häuschen aus eine geräumige Terrassenplattform, auf der die Bewohner ihren einmaligen Blick ins Land abschreiten. Der Holzbelag der Plattform ist behutsam um mächtige Baumstämme herum verlegt, wodurch das kleine Anwesen sozusagen mit dem Wald verwurzelt ist.

Maison d'été

Cette maison de vacances est un projet personnel des jeunes architectes, et a été construite pour une utilisation strictement privée. Avec cet exercice réalisé sur le bois, ils ont trouvé un langage formel prégnant qui a attiré l'attention des professionnels du secteur et leur a valu d'être invités à de grands concours. Ce petit ensemble se définit par quelques lignes puissantes, et une forme arrondie élégante. C'est le résultat des activités des propriétaires en ce lieu : ils s'installent à la lisière de la forêt pour profiter de la vue grandiose sur le fjord. Le côté arrondi du pavillon donne un appui protecteur, comme un transat confortable. Les résidents peuvent admirer leur vue unique tout en déambulant sur la plateforme de la terrasse spacieuse qui s'étend parallèlement au fjord. Elle a été posée en suivant soigneusement le contour des gros troncs d'arbre, ce qui donne l'impression que la petite maison prend racine dans la forêt.

A second small house is planned
as an expansion to this refuge.

Eine Erweiterung des Refugiums
um ein zweites Häuschen ist
geplant.

Une deuxième petite maison est
prévue en annexe de ce refuge.

The project was the realization of
collaboration between an architecture student and a carpenter.

Das Projekt wurde in Eigenarbeit
zusammen mit einem befreunde-
ten Architekturstudenten und
Tischler realisiert.

Ce projet est une collaboration
amicale entre un étudiant en
architecture et un charpentier.

Viewing Point

Architecture should take second place behind nature at this location – this is the maxim Todd Saunders and Tommie Wilhelmsen set when they took on this project. The beauty of the landscape could hardly be increased through a building, they wrote. Rather, there was the danger of compromising this beauty, and so the viewing platform only hints at stepping forward and looking out and its form is otherwise quite minimal. The construction of steel beams and cables was covered on all sides with pressure-treated pine and as a result seems friendly and light, and not like a foreign object in the landscape. Visitors from around the world have enjoyed this unique view and trusted themselves to advance the 30 meters to the crook of the bridge.

Aussichtspunkt

Architektur solle an diesem Platz hinter die Natur zurücktreten – diese Maxime hatten sich Todd Saunders und Tommie Wilhelmsen für das Projekt in Aurland, Norwegen, gesetzt. Die Schönheit der Landschaft könne hier durch etwas Gebautes kaum gesteigert werden, schreiben sie. Eher bestünde die Gefahr, diese Schönheit zu beeinträchtigen. So vollzieht die Aussichtsplattform nur den Gestus des Vortretens und Hinausschauens nach, ist in ihrer Form sonst ganz reduziert. Die Konstruktion aus Stahlträgern und -seilen wurde allseitig mit druckimprägniertem Pinienholz verkleidet und wirkt dadurch freundlich und hell und nicht wie ein Fremdkörper in der Landschaft. Besucher aus aller Welt haben mittlerweile die einzigartige Aussicht genossen und sich die gut 30 m bis zum Knie der Brücke vorgewagt.

Point de vue

Sur ce site, l'architecture doit s'effacer devant la nature. C'est la maxime que Todd Saunders et Tommie Wilhelmsen ont adoptée pour ce projet. Aucune structure ne pourrait vraiment accentuer la beauté de ce paysage, ont-ils écrit. Le risque était plutôt d'altérer cette beauté. La plateforme d'observation se contente donc de suggérer le geste de s'avancer et de regarder, et est par ailleurs minimaliste dans sa forme. La structure en poutres et câbles d'acier a été revêtue de toutes parts avec du pin traité sous pression, ce qui lui donne une allure conviviale et légère et lui évite de donner l'impression d'être un corps étranger dans le paysage. Des visiteurs des quatre coins du globe ont profité de cette vue magnifique et se sont aventurés sur les 30 mètres qui mènent jusqu'au coude du pont.

Strong tensile forces are at work at the outermost point of the bridge, countered through steel cables in the interior of the construction.

Am äußersten Punkt der Brücke wirken starke Zugkräfte, die durch Stahlseile im Inneren der Konstruktion aufgefangen werden.

Les tensions puissantes à l'œuvre à l'extrémité du pont sont domptées par les câbles en acier de l'intérieur de la structure.

Posbank Tea Pavilion

The Posbank Pavilion is a visitor center with a tearoom in Nationalpark Veluwe Zoom Rheden in the Netherlands. The building makes the surrounding nature, natural history and ecology subjects for discussion. It was built around ice-age moraine rises and is centered on one of these hills. The outer parts of the room are spiral-shaped and even encircle a small group of trees that was preserved during building. All of the load-bearing building elements consist of whole tree trunks – these are unfinished massive oaks. The horizontal building elements are made of steel, the shell is of glass, and the flat roofs are planted. The building is low-energy use. In the interior, the ceiling and floor coverings take up the idea of mimicry: a parquet of wood discs and the finest sheets of wood veneer hanging from the ceiling fit with ease in the light, wooded forest surroundings.

Posbank Teepavillon

Der Posbank Pavillon ist Besucherhaus mit Teestube im Nationalpark Veluwe Zoom Rheden (Niederlande). Der Bau thematisiert die umgebende Natur, Naturgeschichte und Ökologie. Er wurde um eiszeitliche Moränenerhebungen herum errichtet und setzt in seinem Zentrum auf einen dieser Hügel auf. Die äußeren Raumteile sind spiralförmig angelegt und umschließen außerdem eine kleine Baumgruppe, die bei der Bebauung erhalten bleiben sollte. Alle tragenden Konstruktionselemente bestehen aus ganzen Baumstämmen – es handelt sich um unbehandelte massive Eiche. Die horizontalen Bauteile bestehen aus Stahl, die Hülle aus Glas und die Flachdächer sind begrünt. Das Gebäude wurde dabei als Niedrigenergiesystem realisiert. Im Inneren nehmen die Decken- und Bodenverkleidungen die Mimesisidee auf: Ein Holzscheibenparkett und von der Decke hängende feinste Holzfurnierblätter fügen sich harmonisch in die lichte Bewaldung der Umgebung ein.

Pavillon du thé de Posbank

Le pavillon de Posbank est un centre doté d'un salon de thé, consacré aux visiteurs du parc national de Veluwe Zoom, à Rheden (Pays-Bas). Le bâtiment traite des thèmes de la nature environnante, de l'histoire naturelle et de l'écologie. Il a été construit sur des moraines de l'ère glaciaires, et est centré sur l'un de ces monticules. Les parties extérieures forment une spirale et entourent un petit bosquet que le chantier devait épargner. Tous les éléments porteurs de la construction sont constitués des troncs bruts de grands chênes. Les éléments horizontaux sont en acier, l'enveloppe extérieure est en verre, et les toits plats sont couverts de végétaux. La consommation d'énergie du bâtiment est très faible. À l'intérieur, le plafond et le sol reprennent l'idée du mimétisme : les disques en bois du parquet et les fines plaques de bois qui pendent du plafond se fondent dans le paysage de bois clairsemés.

Tree houses belong to the theme of architecture and wood – and the Posbank Pavilion integrates living trees.

Zum Thema Architektur und Holz gehören Baumhäuser – auch der Posbank Pavillon integriert lebende Bäume.

Les maisons dans les arbres ont leur place dans le thème de l'architecture et du bois, et le pavillon de Posbank comprend des arbres vivants.

De Wolzak House

This project, restoring and expanding an old farmstead, was intended to reflect the diverse lives and interests of the new owners – a large family and their guests – through different architectural ideas. Lively contrasts shape the appearance of the farmstead. The old building with traditional brick walls and thatched roof contrasts with the unusual shapes of the new building. Its roof area shows a patchwork of different lattice patterns consisting of wood slats of varying sizes. The glass surfaces organized behind and between them follow no system. One section of the building is also covered in glass in the roof area, so that a substructure of naturally growing tree trunks is visible. These create a clear contrast with the straight lines of the adjacent wooden shutters. Wood also dominates the interior. Unconcealed massive board walls that were created individually influence the room's impression.

Haus De Wolzak

Bei diesem Projekt der Sanierung und Erweiterung eines alten Bauernhofes sollte die Vielfalt der Lebensbereiche der neuen Bewohner – einer großen Familie und ihrer Gäste – durch unterschiedlichste Architekturideen sichtbar gemacht werden. Lebhafte Kontraste prägen das Erscheinungsbild der Gebäudeanlage. Der Altbau im traditionellen Kleid mit Ziegelwand und Reetdach kontrastiert mit den ungewöhnlichen Formen des Neubaus. Dessen Dachzone stellt ein Patchwork verschiedenster Holzlattenmuster dar, die mit unterschiedlich großen Leistenabständen verlegt wurden. Die dahinter und dazwischen angeordneten Glasflächen folgen keinem System. Ein Gebäudeabschnitt ist auch im Dachbereich verglast, so dass seine Unterkonstruktion aus naturgewachsenen Baumstämmen sichtbar wird. Diese bilden einen deutlichen Gegensatz zu den benachbarten geradlinigen Holzlamellen. In den Innenräumen dominiert ebenfalls Holz. Unverkleidete, massive Tafelwände, die individuell vorgefertig wurden, prägen den Raumeindruck.

Maison De Wolzak

Ce projet de restauration et d'agrandissement d'une vieille ferme devait exprimer la diversité des vies et des intérêts des propriétaires, une grande famille et ses invités, à travers plusieurs idées architecturales. L'aspect extérieur est fait de contrastes dynamiques. L'ancien bâtiment aux murs de briques et au toit en chaume tranche avec les formes inhabituelles du nouveau bâtiment. Le toit est un patchwork de différents motifs quadrillés que forment des lattes de dimensions diverses. Les surfaces vitrées organisées derrière et entre ces motifs ne suivent aucun système particulier. Une partie du toit est également vitrée, et dévoile une ossature en troncs d'arbres bruts. Ils créent un contraste saisissant avec les lignes bien droites des lattes voisines. L'intérieur est lui aussi dominé par le bois. Les murs revêtus de panneaux préfabriqués individuellement donnent le ton.

Both inside and outside things were purposely built slightly askew, thereby taking into account the rustic, historical location.

Innen wie außen hat man absichtlich ein wenig windschief gebaut und damit doch dem rustikalen historischen Ort Rechnung getragen.

À l'intérieur comme à l'extérieur, les différents éléments ont été plantés légèrement de guingois, en harmonie avec ce lieu rustique et historique.

A winter garden has sprung up between the old and new buildings.

Zwischen den alten und neuen Gebäudeteilen ist ein Wintergarten entstanden.

Un jardin d'hiver a trouvé sa place entre l'ancien bâtiment et le nouveau.

Regina Schineis

Music Practice Chamber

Wood as a building material with good acoustical properties was the central idea of the practice chamber. Wood was also used to build the neighboring musician's home. The sanded surface of the interior paneling is unfinished, further enhancing the acoustics. It is unusual though that the up-thrust areas of the walls and ceilings, which also optimize the acoustics, are carried through to the outside. Although it consists of only one room, the building became a highly malleable object, emphasized by its nearly free-soaring serrated contour. The folds of glue-laminated timber were completely covered with copper cassettes, a material whose color and natural glow harmonizes well with wood.

Musikprobensaal

Holz als klangfreundliches Baumaterial lag bei der Konzeption des Probenraumes nahe. Auch im benachbarten Musikerheim wurde mit Holz gebaut. Die geschliffene Oberfläche der Innenraumverkleidung ist unversiegelt, was eine weitere Verbesserung der Akustik mit sich bringt. Ungewöhnlich ist jedoch, dass die Auffaltung der Wände und Decken, die sich ebenfalls aus der Schalloptimierung herleitet, auf der Außenseite des Gebäudes beibehalten wurde. Obwohl nur aus einem einzelnen Raum bestehend, wird der Bau somit zu einem hochplastischen Körper, was noch betont wird durch die nahezu frei schwebende gezackte untere Gebäudekante. Das Faltwerk aus Brettschichtholzelementen wurde außen vollständig mit vorgehängten Kupferkassetten ummantelt, einem Material, das in seiner Farbigkeit und natürlichen Ausstrahlung sehr gut mit Holz harmoniert.

Studio de répétition

C'est le bois, et ses propriétés acoustiques, qui est au centre du concept de ce studio de répétition. Il a également été utilisé pour construire la maison voisine du musicien. À l'intérieur, la surface poncée des panneaux a été laissée telle quelle, ce qui améliore encore l'acoustique. Il est cependant inhabituel que les éléments porteurs saillants des murs et du plafond, qui participent également à l'acoustique, soient prolongés à l'extérieur du bâtiment. Bien qu'il n'ait qu'une seule pièce, ce bâtiment est très flexible, caractéristique soulignée par son contour zigzagant et presque flottant. Le voile plissé en bois lamellé-collé a été complètement revêtu de caissons en cuivre, un matériau dont la couleur et les reflets naturels s'harmonisent parfaitement avec le bois.

The glue-laminated timber for the folded shape of walls and ceiling was prefabricated.

Die Brettschichtholztafeln für die Faltenform von Wänden und Decke wurden im Werk vorgefertigt.

Les panneaux lamellés-collés des murs et du plafond plissés ont été préfabriqués.

The dark metal on the vertical window supports recedes visually to the advantage of the horizontal stripes of the wooden crossbeams.

Das dunkle Metall der senkrechten Fensterstützen tritt optisch zugunsten des hölzernen Streifenmusters der Querstreben zurück.

Le métal sombre des supports verticaux de la baie vitrée s'efface devant les bandes horizontales des traverses en bois.

On its short sides, the one-room building is covered completely in glass, allowing a view to the green surroundings.

An seinen Kurzseiten ist das einräumige Gebäude komplett verglast und man blickt in eine begrünte Umgebung.

L'avant du bâtiment est totalement vitré, et donne vue sur la verdure environnante.

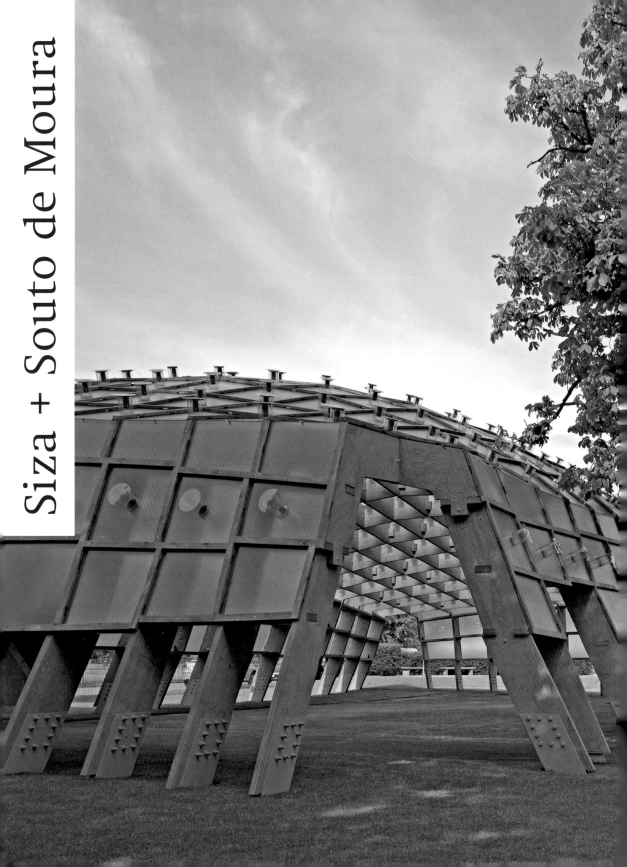

Siza + Souto de Moura

Serpentine Gallery Pavilion

The modular interlocking elements of the construction form a flowing pattern, which continues through the walls and arches. The structure of the wooden mesh is not rigid, but acts like a net made from pliantly formable material, making possible the smooth wave-shaped design. The mesh has an anomalous quality because it has offset and irregular lines instead of right angles. The structure is the third architectural pavilion to be erected in the Serpentine Gallery park in London. It came into being through a collaboration between the engineers from Arup led by Cecil Balmond and the specialist wood construction company Finnforest Merk. The innovative construction is unlike any of the architects' previous work. The materials used included matt polycarbonate for the transparent skin and Kerto®-wood. Kerto® is a homogenized wooden construction material made from spruce. It is processed into a laminated veneer, which increases its strength and elasticity.

Serpentine Gallery Pavillon

Die modularen Steckelemente der Konstruktion bilden ein Raster, aus dem Wände und Gewölbe in einem Zug geformt wurden. Die Struktur des Holzgitters ist nicht starr, sondern verhält sich wie ein Netz aus weich formbarem Material und ermöglicht eine sanft gewellte Form. Weil das Raster Versprünge und schräge Linien statt rechter Winkel aufweist, wirkt es so ungewöhnlich. Der Bau ist der dritte Architekturpavillon, der im Park der Serpentine Gallery London errichtet wurde. In Zusammenarbeit mit Ingenieuren von Arup um Cecil Balmond und dem Spezialisten für Holzbau Finnforest Merk entstand hier eine innovative Konstruktion, die zudem ohne Vorbild im bisherigen Werk der Architekten ist. Die Baustoffe sind mattes Polykarbonat als lichtdurchlässige Verkleidung und Kerto®-Holz. Kerto® ist ein homogenisierter Holzwerkstoff aus Fichte. Durch die Verarbeitung zu Furnierschichtholz wurde seine Festigkeit und Elastizität extrem erhöht.

Pavillon de la Serpentine Gallery

Les éléments modulaires fichés les uns dans les autres dessinent un quadrillage qui donne forme aux murs et à la voûte du bâtiment d'un seul trait. La structure de la grille en bois n'est pas rigide, elle se comporte plutôt comme un filet souple et malléable qui permet un mouvement doux et ondulant. Ce sont les lignes du quadrillage, décalées et en biais au lieu de se rencontrer à angle droit, qui lui confèrent son aspect si inhabituel. Il s'agit du troisième pavillon d'architecture construit dans le parc de la Serpentine Gallery de Londres. De la collaboration avec les ingénieurs d'Arup, menés par Cecil Balmond, et l'équipe de spécialistes de la construction en bois de Finnforest Merk est né un bâtiment innovant, sans exemple comparable dans les travaux précédents des architectes. Les matériaux employés sont un revêtement en polycarbonate qui laisse passer la lumière et du bois Kerto®. Le Kerto® est composé de bois de sapin rouge homogénéisé. Le traitement de ce bois lamifié a considérablement augmenté ses qualités de solidité et d'élasticité.

Snøhetta

Oslo Opera House

The different materials envisaged for use in the initial planning stage became a source of inspiration for the architects over the entire project. The focus was on three main, but converse materials. These are symbolically bound to the three main themes of the building. Wood is used for the so-called "Wave Wall" – a house inside the opera house. It comprises of an auditorium at the center and ring-shapes spaces around it. The wood used was oak, which was treated with ammonia, darkening its color in places. Several floors high, this organically curved wooden "Wave Wall" appears monumental. It forms the visual facade of the opera house as seen from the sea and is composed of a complex of interwoven curves and openings. The surface of the outer skin is not flat, it features a functional acoustic relief. Here, the organic and geometric forms react with one another.

Opernhaus Oslo

Für die Architekten war das planerische Spiel mit verschiedenen Materialien Inspirationsquelle für das gesamte Projekt. Man konzentrierte sich auf drei gegensätzliche Hauptmaterialien. Diese sind symbolisch mit drei Hauptthemen des Gebäudes verbunden. Holz ist das Material der „Wave Wall" – des Haus-im-Haus der Oper. Es besteht aus dem Auditorium im Zentrum und den es ringförmig umgebenden Räumlichkeiten. Das Material ist Eichenholz, welches durch die Behandlung mit Ammoniak stellenweise dunkel eingefärbt wurde. Als mehrere Stockwerke hohe, organisch geschwungene Wand aus Holz wirkt die „Wave Wall" monumental. Sie bildet die Sichtfassade der Oper zum Meer hin und wurde durch komplex miteinander verflochtene Schwünge und Öffnungen gegliedert. Die Oberfläche der Verkleidung ist nicht glatt, sondern weist ein Relief auf, das auch akustischen Zwecken dient. Organische und geometrische Formen reagieren hier aufeinander.

Opéra d'Oslo

Pour les architectes, c'est le jeu de l'organisation autour de différents matériaux qui a inspiré le projet dans son ensemble. Ils se sont concentrés sur trois matériaux principaux qui créent des contrastes tranchés et correspondent symboliquement aux trois « thèmes principaux » du bâtiment. Le bois est le matériau du « Wave Wall », le noyau de l'Opéra. Il est constitué de l'auditorium au centre, entouré d'espaces disposés en anneau. Le matériau utilisé est le chêne, traité à l'ammoniaque par endroits pour lui faire prendre une teinte plus sombre. Le « Wave Wall » est un mur en bois aux courbes organiques qui s'élève sur plusieurs étages et s'impose comme un véritable monument. Il forme la façade de l'Opéra qui donne sur la mer et sa structure est un jeu complexe d'ouvertures et de mouvements entrecroisés. Sa surface n'est pas lisse, mais présente au contraire des reliefs qui remplissent également des fonctions acoustiques. Ici, les formes organiques et géométriques se répondent les unes aux autres.

Stained and polished oak was used in the auditorium. In the foyer, on the other hand, is an open-pored, matt surface.

Gebeiztes und poliertes Eichenholz wurde im Zuschauerraum verarbeitet. Im Foyer hingegen zeigt es eine offenporige, matte Oberfläche.

L'auditorium a été réalisé en chêne teinté et poli. Dans le foyer, les surfaces sont en revanche mates et la matière brute respire.

The wooden interior architecture of the foyer tends toward generous curved shapes, while the building's exterior is surrounded by angular glass and marble ramps.

Die hölzerne Innenarchitektur des Foyers verläuft in großzügig geschwungenen Formen, während das Gebäude außen von eckigen Glas-Marmor-Rampen umschlossen wird.

L'architecture en bois de l'intérieur du foyer affiche des courbes généreuses, tandis que l'extérieur du bâtiment est dominé par les angles du verre et des rampes en marbre.

The size of the "Wave Wall" is shown to its best advantage looking from outside into the lighted opera house.

Die Größe der „Wave Wall" (Wellenwand) kommt besonders beim Blick von außen in das beleuchtete Opernhaus zur Geltung.

C'est de l'extérieur de l'opéra éclairé que l'on apprécie le mieux les dimensions du « Wave Wall ».

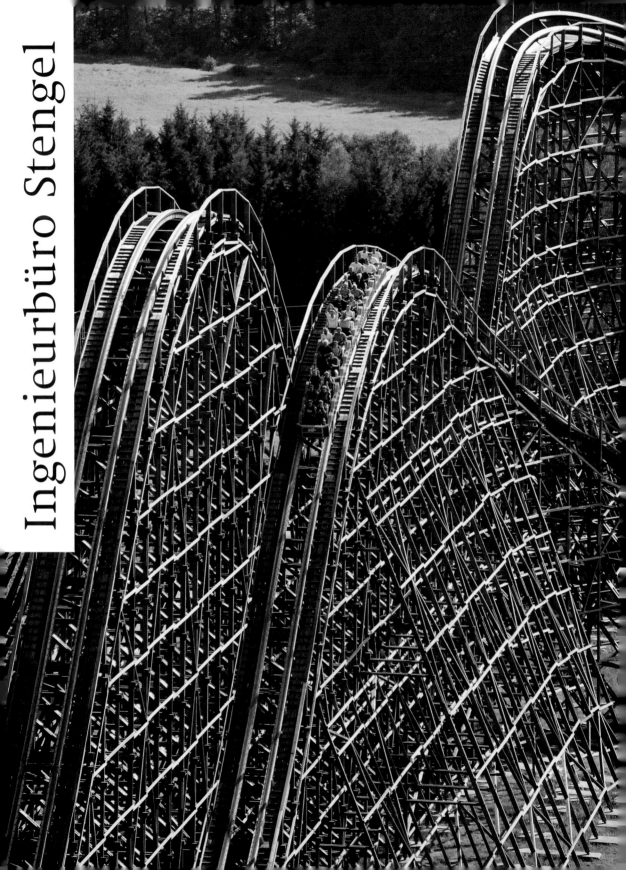

Ingenieurbüro Stengel

Wood Roller Coaster Colossos

Less-courageous visitors to the roller coaster will be relieved to know that a good half of all roller coasters worldwide were designed and built by the Werner Stengel office. Wooden thrill rides are actually rare, but continue to be built in the 21st century because of their beauty, especially when they are situated in front of natural backdrops. For a time Colossos held the record for being the largest and steepest wood roller coaster in the world. The mountain and valley tracks are built on a load-bearing structure of pine beams, reinforcements and extremely long struts. The material requires special care: it must constantly be kept damp so it does not tear. The specialists in large wood structures, Intamin and Cordes, built the Colossos roller coaster for the Heath-Park Soltau. It consists of 90,000 individual wood parts, of which 20,000 are unique.

Holzachterbahn Colossos

Weniger wagemutige Besucher der Achterbahn wird es beruhigen zu wissen, dass gut die Hälfte aller Achterbahnen weltweit durch das Büro Werner Stengel konstruiert und realisiert wurden. Fahrgeschäfte aus Holz sind eher selten, werden jedoch auch im 21. Jahrhundert noch wegen ihrer Schönheit erbaut, besonders wenn sie vor einer Naturkulisse stehen. Colossos war vorübergehend Rekordhalter als international größte und steilste Holzachterbahn. Die Berg- und Talfahrten werden von einem Tragwerk aus Kiefernholzbalken, dichten Aussteifungen und extrem langen Abstrebungen gehalten. Das Material bedarf besonderer Pflege: Es muss permanent feucht gehalten werden, damit es nicht reißt. Die Spezialisten für Holzgroßbauten Intamin und Cordes realisierten die Colossos-Achterbahn für den Heide-Park Soltau. Sie besteht aus 90.000 Holzeinzelteilen; darunter 20.000 unterschiedliche Teile.

Montagnes russes en bois Colossos

Les visiteurs les moins téméraires seront soulagés d'apprendre qu'une bonne moitié des montagnes russes de la planète ont été conçues et construites par le cabinet Werner Stengel. Les exemplaires en bois sont en fait assez rares, mais ils sont encore construits au XXIe siècle car ils sont d'une grande beauté, surtout lorsqu'ils sont plantés dans un décor naturel. Colossos a pendant un temps détenu le record de la montagne russe la plus grande et la plus escarpée du monde. Les montées et les descentes sont construites sur une structure faite de poutres en pin, d'entretoises épaisses et d'étais extrêmement longs. Le matériau nécessite un entretien spécial : il doit être constamment humidifié afin d'éviter les fissures. Ce sont les spécialistes des grandes structures en bois Intamin et Cordes qui ont construit les montagnes russes du Colossos pour le Heide-Park de Soltau. Elles consistent de 90 000 pièces de bois de 20 000 types différents.

The roller coaster's tracks are made in part from wood and every wood curve was formed accurate to the millimeter using computer-aided production.

Der Schienenweg der Achterbahn besteht in Teilen auch aus Holz, wobei jede Holzrundung durch computergesteuerte Produktion millimetergenau geformt wurde.

Les voies de cette attraction sont en partie faites de bois, et chaque courbe a été façonnée au millimètre près grâce à un procédé de production assistée par ordinateur.

Bernard Tschumi

18

Concert Hall

The new concert hall in French Limoges lies in a thickly wooded area with trees up to 200 years old. Bernard Tschumi worked here to create an ecologically correct construction, made primarily of local building materials and in harmony with the landscape. The interior rooms of the venue are finished entirely in wood, as the case should be for a music stage. Surrounding these are two snail-shaped outer shells made of increasingly lighter wood substructures. A cover of semi-transparent, recyclable polycarbonate film is stretched over these substructures.

Konzerthalle

Die neue Konzerthalle im französischen Limoges liegt in einem dicht bewaldeten Gebiet mit bis zu 200 Jahre altem Baumbestand. Bernard Tschumi strebte hier eine ökologisch korrekte, auf lokale Baumaterialien konzentrierte und landschaftlich harmonisierende Konstruktion an. Die Innenräume der Veranstaltungs-stätte sind vollständig mit Holz ausgekleidet, wie es sich für eine Musikbühne gehört. Um diese herum liegen schneckenhausförmig zwei äußere Hüllen mit zunehmend lichter werdender Holzunterkonstruktion. Darüber spannt sich eine Hülle aus mattdurchsichtiger, recycelbarer Polykarbonatfolie.

Salle de concert

La nouvelle salle de concert de Limoges se dresse sur un terrain très boisé qui compte des arbres vieux de deux siècles. Ici, Bernard Tschumi s'est attaché à concevoir un bâtiment écologique, réalisé à partir de matériaux locaux et en harmonie avec le paysage. Les salles sont entièrement habillées de bois, comme il sied aux endroits consacrés à la musique. Elles sont entourées par deux coques extérieures en colimaçon dont l'ossature en bois recherche la légèreté. Cette ossature est recouverte d'un film translucide en polycarbonate recyclable.

The use of two-by-fours corresponds to a type of masonry on the interior wall surfaces.

Die Verwendung von Kanthölzern entspricht bei den innen aufgehenden Wandflächen einer Art Mauerwerk.

Sur les surfaces des murs internes, l'utilisation de bois équarri correspond à un type de construction.

The same principle was followed for the paneling on the underside of the auditorium proscenium arc.

Das gleiche Prinzip wurde zur Verkleidung der Unterseite des Auditoriumstrichters genutzt.

Le même principe a été appliqué pour les panneaux sous le proscenium de l'auditorium.

The building's transparent bubble of an exterior relieves the hall of any weight.

Der transparente Ballon der Gebäudeaußenhaut nimmt der Halle jegliche Schwere.

La bulle transparente qui entoure l'édifice lui confère une grande légèreté.

Peter Zumthor

Swiss Expo Pavilion
Hanover 2000

Peter Zumthor, prizewinner of the Spirit of Nature Wood Architecture Award and self-taught cabinetmaker, has radical ideas about wood. He once described wood architecture as "a vision of massive blocks of wood as big as a house, a dense volume of horizontal, regularly hewn layers". On the occasion of the Expo 2000 he realized this vision and created more of a work of art. There is something very unstructured about this 'architecture': the Pavilion consists of twelve layers of fresh-cut larch and pine beams. The wooden pieces are held in place only by their own weight and by tie rod and spacers. Rooms reveal themselves between the mazelike seven-meter-tall and 50-meter-long walls. The analogy to stacks of wood in a lumberyard is intentional.

EXPO-Pavillon Schweiz
Hannover 2000

Peter Zumthor, Preisträger des Spirit of Nature Wood Architecture Award und selbst gelernter Kunsttischler, trägt radikale Vorstellungen vom Material Holz in sich. Er beschrieb Holzarchitektur einmal als die „Vision eines massiven Holzblocks von der Größe eines Hauses, eines dichten Volumens aus horizontalen, nach regelmäßigen Formen behauenen Schichten." Diese Vision hat er anlässlich der Expo 2000 realisiert und dabei eher ein Kunstobjekt erschaffen. Es steckt in dieser „Architektur" etwas sehr Ungebautes: Der Pavillon besteht aus zwölf Stapeln frisch geschnittener Lärchen- und Föhrenholzbalken. Die Holzpakete werden lediglich von ihrem Eigengewicht und von Zugstangen gehalten; sie sind also nur verschnürt. Zwischen den labyrinthartig gestellten, je 7 m hohen und 50 m langen Wänden tun sich Räume auf. Die Analogie zu Bretterstapeln in einem Holzlager ist beabsichtigt.

Pavillon de la Suisse à l'EXPO de
Hanovre 2000

Peter Zumthor, lauréat du prix Spirit of Nature Wood Architecture, est un ébéniste autodidacte qui a des idées radicales sur le bois. Il a un jour décrit l'architecture en bois avec ces mots : « une vision de blocs de bois massifs aussi grands qu'une maison, un volume dense de couches horizontales et régulières. » Il a réalisé cette vision à l'occasion de l'Expo 2000 et le résultat tient davantage de l'œuvre d'art. Cette « architecture » a quelque chose de très déstructuré : le pavillon se compose de douze piles de poutres fraîchement débitées de pin et de mélèze. C'est leur propre poids qui leur confère leur stabilité, ainsi que des barres d'ancrage. Les salles surgissent au détour des murs de 7 mètres de hauteur et 50 mètres de longueur dignes d'un labyrinthe. Le fait que les piles de planches semblent appartenir à un dépôt de bois n'est pas un hasard.

The country pavilion was played as a 'sound box Switzerland.' Changing improvised musical performances were held in the wood maze.

Der Länderpavillon wurde als „Klangkörper Schweiz" bespielt. Im Holzlabyrinth fanden wechselnde, improvisierte Musikperformances statt.

Le pavillon a fait office de « boîte à musique suisse ». Le labyrinthe en bois a accueilli diverses représentations musicales improvisées.

No other Expo building so closely met the organizers' requirement for materials to be reusable: the unfinished wood could be returned to the open market.

Kein anderes Expogebäude setzte so konsequent die Auflage der Veranstalter nach Wiederverwertbarkeit um: Das unbearbeitete Holz konnte wieder dem Markt zugeführt werden.

Aucun autre pavillon de l'Expo n'a rempli aussi bien le critère fixé par l'organisation sur la réutilisation des matériaux après l'événement : le bois non traité a été remis directement sur le marché.

The large screw clamps of the wiring and the protruding rain gutters of the roof strengthened the impression of a warehouse.

Die großen Schraubzwingen der Verdrahtung und die weit überstehenden Regenrinnen des Daches verstärken die Anmutung eines Materiallagers.

Les gros serre-câbles et les gouttières saillantes du toit renforcent l'impression de se trouver dans un entrepôt.

Luzi House

As close as the architectural debate about the theme of wood comes to the idea of ancient building techniques, so little does the simple adaptation of those techniques function. Zumthor had to solve the problem of too little window space in his project of building a private home using the Strickbau technique. Zumthor focused his creative energy as much as possible on the corners of the house, and was able to open the walls between them for large windows. Panoramas of up to six meters in width became possible. Strickbau's insertion principle of building with no need for screws, wall anchors, nails, etc. was also applied around the vertical window hinges. Each side of the house was further braced and deep extensions over the balconies protect against wind.

Haus Luzi

So nahe wie bei der architektonischen Auseinandersetzung mit dem Thema Holz die Bezugnahme auf uralte Bauweisen liegt, so wenig funktioniert die schlichte Adaption derselben. Für Zumthors Projekt eines Privathauses in sogenannter Strickbautechnik galt es, das Problem mangelnder Fensterflächen zu lösen. Im Ergebnis konzentrierte Zumthor alle konstruktiven Kräfte so nahe wie möglich um die Hausecken herum und konnte so die dazwischen liegenden Wände für große Fenster öffnen. Bis zu 6 m breite Panoramen ergeben sich so. Das Steckprinzip des Strickbaus findet dabei auch rund um die vertikalen Fensterbänder Anwendung. Damit erhält jede Hausseite eine zusätzliche Aussteifung und die weit vorgezogenen Balkenüberstände schützen gegen Wind.

Maison Luzi

Les techniques de construction ancestrales ont beau être au cœur du débat sur le bois dans l'architecture, leur application est loin d'être simple. Pour ce projet de maison individuelle en madriers carrés selon la technique du Strickbau, Peter Zumthor devait résoudre le problème du manque de surface pour les fenêtres. Il a concentré son énergie créative sur les coins de la maison, et a ainsi réussi à percer de grandes fenêtres dans les murs, ce qui s'est traduit par des panoramiques de jusqu'à 6 mètres de largeur. Le principe d'encastrement du Strickbau a également été appliqué autour des charnières verticales des fenêtres. Chaque côté de la maison est renforcé, et les balcons sont dotés de véritables toits qui protègent du vent.

The so-called Strickbau technique is a Swiss variation on the log cabin. Here also the walls are made of layered and mortised solid beams ('knitted').

Der sogenannte Strickbau ist eine schweizerische Variante des Blockhausbaus. Auch hier werden Wände aus geschichteten und verzapften massiven Balken errichtet („gestrickt").

La technique du Strickbau (du verbe stricken, qui signifie trico-ter) est une variante suisse de la maison en rondins. Les murs sont faits de poutres massives empilées et encastrées.

Index | Verzeichnis

Directory

24H-architecture
Rotterdam, The Netherlands
www.24h-architecture.com
Photos: Christian Richters

Aequo
Assen, The Netherlands
www.aequo.nl
Photos: Erik Hemsberg, Jan Bartelsman

Will Alsop
London, United Kingdom
www.alsoparchitects.com
Photos: © SMC Alsop/Richard Johnson

Banz + Riecks
Bochum, Germany
www.banz-riecks.de
Photos: Holzabsatzfonds, Bonn

Berger + Parkkinen
Helsinki, Finland
www.berger-parkkinen.com
Photos: Christian Richters

Klaus Block
Berlin, Germany
www.klausblock.de
Photos: Holzabsatzfonds, Bonn

Bonte & Migozzi
Marseille, France
www.architectes.org/portfolios/
bonte-migozzi-architectes
Photos: Foto Cabanel, Foto F. Joliot

Gianni Botsford Architects
London, United Kingdom
www.giannibotsford.com
Photos: Christian Richters

Gion A. Caminada
Vrin, Switzerland
Photos: Christian Richters

Edward Cullinan Architects
London, United Kingdom
www.edwardcullinanarchitects.com
Photos: Richard Learoyd

Farwick + Grote
Ahaus, Germany
www.farwickgrote.de
Photos: Holzabsatzfonds, Bonn

FOA ForeignOfficeArchitects
London, United Kingdom
www.f-o-a.net
Photos: Satoru Mishima

Gassner & Zarecky
Munich, Germany
www.gassner-zarecky.de
Photos: Gassner & Zarecky

Frank O. and Samuel Gehry
Los Angeles, USA
www.gehrypartners.com
Photos: Christian Richters

Ville Hara, avanto arkkitehdit
Helsinki, Finland
www.avan.to
Photos: Jussi Tianinen, HUT photolab

Hentrich-Petschnigg & Partner
Düsseldorf, Germany
www.hpp.com
Photos: Hentrich-Petschnigg & Partner

Thomas Herzog
Munich, Germany
www.herzog-und-partner.de
Photos: Christian Richters

Heydorn.Eaton.Architekten
Berlin, Germany
www.heydorneaton.de
Photos: Holzabsatzfonds, Bonn

Jensen & Skodvin
Oslo, Norway
www.jsa.no
Photos: Jensen & Skodvin Arkitekt-
kontor

Daniel Libeskind
New York, USA
www.daniel-libeskind.com
Photos: Christian Richters

McCullough Mulvin
Dublin, Ireland
www.mcculloughmulvin.com
Photos: Christian Richters

MGF Mahler Günster Fuchs
Stuttgart, Germany
www.mgf-architekten.de
Photos: (Hochschule für Wirtschaft
und Technik) Christian Richters
(Fakultät für Gestaltung) Christian
Richters, OKALUX/ © Ali Moshiri

Nils Holger Moormann
Aschau, Germany
www.moormann.de
Photos: Nils Holger Moormann (berge)
Jäger & Jäger (Walden)

MVRDV
Rotterdam, The Netherlands
www.mvrdv.nl
Photos: Christian Richters

Nägeliarchitekten
Berlin, Germany
www.naegeliarchitekten.de
Photos: Holzabsatzfonds, Bonn

Renzo Piano
Genova, Italy
www.rpbw.com
© Centre Culturel Tjibaou-ADCK
Photos: rpbw/John Gollings

Petzinka Pink
Düsseldorf, Germany
www.petzinka-pink.de
Photos: Holzabsatzfonds, Bonn

Rudolf Reitermann und
Peter Sassenroth
Berlin, Germany
Photos: Holzabsatzfonds, Bonn

Richard Rogers
London, United Kingdom
www.richardrogers.co.uk
Photos: Christian Richters

sauerbruch hutton architekten
Berlin, Germany
www.sauerbruchhutton.de
Photos: Christian Richters

Saunders & Wilhelmsen
www.saunders-wilhelmsen.no
Photos: Bent René Synnevåg
(Hardanger)
Todd Saunders, Nils Vik (Aurland)

SeArch
Amsterdam, The Netherlands
www.search.nl
Photos: Christian Richters

Regina Schineis
Augsburg, Germany
www.schineis.com
Photos: Holzabsatzfonds, Bonn

Siza + Souto de Moura
www.serpentinegallery.org
Photos: © Serpentine Gallery/Richard
Bryant

Snøhetta
Oslo, Norway
www.snoarc.no
Photos: Christian Richters

Ingenieurbüro Stengel
www.rcstengel.com
www.cordes-row.de
Photos: Holzabsatzfonds, Bonn

Bernard Tschumi
New York, USA
www.tschumi.com
Photos: Christian Richters

Peter Zumthor
Haldenstein, Switzerland
arch@zumthor.ch
Photos: Christian Richters

© 2009 Tandem Verlag GmbH
h.f.ullmann is an imprint of
Tandem Verlag GmbH

Research, Text and Editorial:
Barbara Linz
Layout:
Ilona Buchholz, Köln
Design concept:
Klett Fischer
architecture + design publishing
Produced by:
ditter.projektagentur gmbh
www.ditter.net

Project coordination
for h.f.ullmann:
Dania D'Eramo

Translation into English:
Sharon Rodgers for Equipo de
Edición S.L., Barcelona
Translation into French:
Aurélie Daniel for Equipo de
Edición S.L., Barcelona

Printed in China

ISBN: 978-3-8331-4890-3

10 9 8 7 6 5 4 3 2 1
X IX VIII VII VI V IV III II I

www.ullmann-publishing.com